THE MYSTERY OF
Emily Dickinson

Books by Laura Benét

The Boy Shelley

Famous American Humorists

Famous American Poets

Famous New England Authors

Famous Poets for Young People

Famous Storytellers for Young People

The Mystery of Emily Dickinson

Stanley, Invincible Explorer

THE MYSTERY

OF

Emily Dickinson

❧

LAURA BENÉT

Illustrated with photographs

DODD, MEAD & COMPANY
NEW YORK

Grateful acknowledgment is made to:

Houghton Mifflin Company for various selections and three poems, "Title Divine," "Is It True? Dear Sue," and "Bumble Bee's Religion," from *The Life and Letters of Emily Dickinson* by Martha Dickinson Bianchi. Copyright 1924 by Martha Dickinson Bianchi. Copyright renewed 1952 by Alfred Leete Hampson. Reprinted by permission of Houghton Mifflin Company.

Houghton Mifflin Company for selections from *Dear Preceptor, The Life and Times of Thomas Wentworth Higginson,* by Anna Mary Wells. Copyright © 1963 by Anna Mary Wells Smith. Reprinted by permission of Houghton Mifflin Company.

Emily Dickinson's letter to the Reverend Edward Everett Hale was taken from *The Letters of Emily Dickinson*, Thomas H. Johnson and Theodora Ward, Editors, The Belknap Press of Harvard University Press, copyright by the President and Fellows of Harvard College, with the permission of the Trustees of Amherst College.

ISBN 0-396-06934-7
Library of Congress Catalog Card Number: 73-19087

Printed in the United States of America
by The Cornwall Press, Cornwall, N. Y.

For Gertrude Schuyler Norton,
   an old and valued friend,

and

   Edward and Betty Pattison,
   who have done so much for me.

   Affectionately,

   The Author

Acknowledgments

The author wishes to express her appreciation to all who have assisted her, and especially to Jay Leyda and Richard B. Sewall.

Contents

Illustrations

The Dickinson homestead. Emily's home from her birth to 1840, and from 1855 until her death.

Dr. Josiah Holland. Friend of the Dickinsons for many years.

Elizabeth Chapin Holland. Wife of Josiah and Emily's friend and correspondent.

Helen Hunt Jackson. Famous author of *Ramona* and friend of Emily.

Edward Bissell Hunt. Helen Hunt Jackson's first husband.

John Langdon Dudley. Husband of Emily's girlhood friend Eliza Coleman.

Otis Lord. Friend of Emily's father; Emily loved him in her later years.

Samuel Bowles. Editor of the *Springfield Republican*; friend of Austin, and of Emily.

Charles Wadsworth. The minister from Philadelphia. Courtesy of Charles Wadsworth, 3rd.

Martha (Mattie) Dickinson. Daughter of Austin and Sue. Later Martha Dickinson Bianchi, she wrote of her famous aunt.

Edward (Ned) Dickinson. Emily's nephew, first son of Austin and Sue.

Thomas Gilbert (Gib) Dickinson. Austin and Sue's second son, who died in childhood.

THE MYSTERY OF

Emily Dickinson

CHAPTER 1

The Beginning

Emily dickinson, the daughter of Edward Dickinson and Emily Norcross, was born on December 10, 1830, in the tiny farming village of Amherst, Massachusetts. Her birthplace, a stately house belonging to her grandfather, Samuel Fowler Dickinson, was said to be the first brick house in the town. Her entire life, with the exception of a year in boarding school, five or six weeks in Washington and Philadelphia, and occasional short visits to Boston, was to be spent within the circle of Amherst's hills, those hills she passionately loved as season succeeded season.

Emily was the middle child. Her brother Austin was a year and a half older and her sister Vinnie (short for Lavinia), two years younger. As a child Emily was probably considered plain as to features. She had auburn hair cut short, the white skin that went with it, and red-brown eyes like her father's. Vinnie was dark and very pretty. Both girls had wit and charm and Vinnie adored Emily. Neither sister had height, but Austin was tall. The three children were devoted to each other, and there was a rather special understanding between Emily and her brother.

Edward Dickinson, their father, a strangely silent man, was a greatly respected lawyer. As Squire Dickinson, he took a foremost part in all the affairs of his community. He was the stern head of his household, where his word was law. He was rarely seen to smile, and once, when he did, his daughter remarked that it was "embarrassing." Even his wife, an exquisite little person, rather fluttering and tremulous in manner, obeyed him as if he were Jehovah. Mr. Dickinson was the head of a God-fearing New England home where family prayers were held every morning, and the whole family worshiped every Sunday in the yellow Congregational Church at least once and sometimes twice. He had but one vanity and that was to drive the fastest horses in town. Deacon Luke Sweetser was his great rival in this taste.

Though Squire Dickinson thought continually of his family's welfare and comfort, he never unbent sufficiently to show affection. He never singled out Emily as his favorite child; yet he bought her a piano that he might hear her play the tunes that he loved, and later on he presented her with a dog almost as big as herself. To know Emily, one must try to understand her father.

Emily loved her gentle mother and tried to be of use to her in every way possible. But she could never discuss with her the many things in which she was most deeply interested. "My mother does not care for thought," she once reflected. Yet, a letter written by her mother as a schoolgirl, to *her* sister Lavinia, shows some of the traits most pronounced in Emily—extreme affection for her family and anxiety for the weeks to pass so she could go home.

Even as a child, Emily had her own terrors concerning religion. The tolling of the heavy church bell alarmed her, as did the height of the pulpit above her head. Sermons delivered by visiting ministers about fire and brimstone terrified her, and she never truly considered herself as one of the chosen. Yet in the period between childhood and girlhood, she wrote: "I have perfect confidence in God and his promises—and yet I know not why. I feel the world has a prominent place in my affections."

The world was certainly in her affections during a trip to Boston in 1846 to visit an aunt—she wrote a friend that she was not really happy, but "contented." She was taken to Mount Auburn, Bunker Hill, and the Chinese Museum. Emily wrote about the two Chinese gentlemen at the museum who had left their country in the interest of breaking the opium-eating habit. She commented, "There is something peculiarly interesting to me in their self-denial."

While in Boston, Emily was also treated to two concerts and a horticultural exhibition. This trip to the city was excitement enough for some time. She had actually been on "top of the State House, and almost everywhere that you can imagine," she marveled.

Emily first attended the West Middle District Public School which was located not far from her home. Though she was kept at home for two whole terms on account of her health, she found enough to interest her there. Her cherished flowers which were always such a real part of her life were as carefully tended as young children. She helped her mother with various household duties and above all learned to make bread. In 1850 she wrote: "Twin loaves of bread have just been born into the world under my auspices,—fine children, the image of their mother." She must have been especially successful as a baker for as time went on her father would eat no bread but hers.

From the public school, Emily, with Vinnie, went on to spend six years in the new Amherst Academy, which boasted sixty-three pupils. Leonard Humphrey, who had been the valedictorian of his class at Amherst College and was only six years older than many of his scholars, had been selected as principal, assisted by Miss Elizabeth Adams, a capable and beloved teacher well known in Amherst.

Emily wrote to her bosom friend, Abiah Root, who had attended school with her at Amherst, that she was studying mental philosophy, Latin, geology, and botany. This last-named study was a pure pleasure to her. She began to make a fine herbarium out of the wildflowers she gathered on the hillsides. In company with other schoolmates who excelled in botany, she won the privilege of going to the college several times a week to attend Professor Edward Hitchcock's lectures on that subject. Then delicate Mr. Humphrey, knowing how this particular pupil pined for good books, lent her several from his personal library which she carefully concealed in her room so that her father would not see them. She and Vinnie also secretly perused Lydia Maria Child's *Letters from New York* which had been left in the thick hedge at their front door by kindly Elbridge Bowdoin, their father's law partner. Mr. Dickinson would never have approved of what he considered such light reading.

During the next year, her sixteenth, Emily had to study very hard to prepare for the goal of her ambition, Mount Holyoke Female Seminary in South Hadley, a superior boarding school chosen by her father, who firmly believed that every girl should have the experience of a good school away from home. So Emily labored over algebra, Euclid, and ecclesiastical history, and reviewed arithmetic. She had quite a precocious mentality but was also at this time sentimental and given to outpourings in letters both to Abiah (whom she called 'Biah) and to a new friend, Susan Gilbert, whom she greatly admired and to whom she gave her confidence, running to her for help when her family failed to understand some of her advanced ideas. Susan was later to marry Emily's brother and become in reality her "Sister Sue."

Many of the happenings of Emily's early life are revealed in her long letters to Abiah, who spent only a short time at school in Amherst and to whom Emily continued to write for many years. Although there are hints, there was not much in the early letters to foreshadow the "different" and strangely retiring person Emily was to become in her later life.

CHAPTER 2

✢

Mount Holyoke Female Seminary

IN THE FALL of 1847, just before her seventeenth birthday, her father drove Emily over the hills to the seminary, presided over by Miss Mary Lyon, whose greatest ambition for her "young ladies" was to train them to be missionaries in foreign fields. Miss Lyon's assistants drove far and near in summer and winter to collect funds for a school that was considered superior to the other young ladies' seminaries and whose fee was only sixty dollars a year because the pupils carried on every item of the domestic work. It is odd that, so far as is known, pious Mr. Dickinson never reflected that his child Emily would certainly not care to become a missionary. That idea had apparently never entered his head.

Edward Dickinson and his daughter parted formally, as he was never seen to kiss. But the tone of voice in which he said, "You will write frequently, Emily?" betrayed his feelings. Miss Lyon warmly welcomed the new pupil and told her she was to share a room with her cousin, Emily Norcross. "Then you will be less homesick," she added kindly.

But Emily was already desperately homesick in this strange

new world of three hundred girls and thought she would die. She wrote to Abiah that she could not be happy away from Amherst because she had "a very dear home."

For three days she had to work on her entrance examinations for which, fortunately, Amherst Academy had thoroughly prepared her. To her great delight she passed in every subject, entered the Second or Middle class of the school, and was assigned to Miss Rebecca Fiske's section. But her comment on her success was: "I never would endure the suspense which I endured during those three days again for all the treasures of the world."

As every boarder helped with the housework, Emily was soon told she would be in the knife and silver circle. Relieved that she was not to cook, she learned that she was to take the knives from the first tier of tables after breakfast and dinner, and wash and polish them until they shone each night. Gradually her homesickness waned, as the atmosphere was friendly and warm. She said often in her letters home that "Miss Lyon and all the teachers try to do all they can for the comfort and happiness of the girls." She was further cheered, after being away from home two weeks, by a flying visit from her brother Austin. He was now a sophomore at Amherst College and caused quite a flutter among the girls when he came, laden with gifts from home. Emily, in thanking him, wrote that she had watched him out of sight and then dashed upstairs to gloat over the cake, gingerbread, pie, peaches, apples, chestnuts, and grapes he had brought. Probably, Mrs. Dickinson, like any mother, had been worrying about the food at the school. But apparently, the girls at Mount Holyoke were well fed, for Emily detailed a menu in one of her letters which included roast veal, potatoes, gravy, squash, bread and butter, and apple dumpling with sauce for dessert.

There were visits from other members of her family, and in one letter Emily wrote out a full list of her hours and occupations:

> At 6 o'clock we all rise. We breakfast at 7. Our study hours begin at 8. At 9 we all meet in Seminary Hall for devotions. At 10¼ I recite a review of Ancient History. . . . At 11, I recite a lesson in Pope's *Essay on Man*. . . . At 12 I practice calisthetics, and at 12¼ read until dinner, which is at 12½, and after dinner, from 1½ until 2, I sing in Seminary Hall. From 2¾ until 3¾ I practise upon the piano. At 3¾ I go to Sections, where we give in all our accounts for the day, including absence, tardiness, communications, breaking silent study hours, receiving company in our rooms, and ten thousand other things which I will not take time or place to mention.

At half-past four all the students went into the Seminary Hall and received advice from Miss Lyon in the form of a lecture. They had supper at six and the first bell to retire rang at a quarter to nine, after a long, quiet study period. Certainly, there was no room for idleness. Any girl not having a legitimate excuse for any failure had a "black mark" placed against her name.

Of course, Emily counted the weeks until she could go home at Thanksgiving time. Thanksgiving was long in coming, but at last it did. Austin called for her on Wednesday with plenty of warm wraps, and the ten-mile drive over the mountain with him was a delight to Emily in spite of the November wind and rain, as well as to Cousin Emily Norcross who accompanied them. All were at the front door to welcome "the returning one, from mother, with tears in her eyes, down to pussy, who tried to look as gracious as was becoming her dignity."

On Thanksgiving Day the reunited family went to church, had a happy holiday dinner, and entertained callers. They had received four invitations out for the evening, only two of which could be accepted, to Emily's great sorrow. After accompanying their parents on one visit, the young people slipped away to another party with their friends, Mr. Dickinson's firm admonition to be home by ten o'clock ringing in their ears. He was waiting for them on their return, and when Emily played and sang a few tunes for him before bedtime he seemed much gratified.

Back to school Emily went on Monday after four perfect days. Of course, she was looking forward to another visit home at Christmas, but she soon lost herself in her new studies, which, she wrote Abiah, were "Silliman's Chemistry and Cutter's Physiology," both interesting. With the second term she also began what was called "English Composition." Her work in this subject was said from the first to have "marked originality."

There was only one cloud on Emily's horizon. She realized that Miss Lyon expected a public declaration of faith from her as well as from the other girls and she did not feel as yet prepared to make it. After various private meetings with those she termed "impenitents," Miss Lyon one morning at devotions addressed the whole school and said: "All young ladies who wish to share that inestimable privilege of becoming Christians will please rise." Every student rose but Emily

Dickinson, who remained quietly in her seat. She received no reprimand, though the girls who were her friends did not entirely understand her attitude. But worse was to come.

The day before Christmas Miss Lyon announced that the school would observe Christmas by a strict fast and meditation. Congregationalists looked upon Christmas as pagan. Years later Austin was to state he had been brought up believing that its celebration was a "joint device of the Devil and the Romish church," while Emily would write that Mr. Dickinson "frowned upon Santa Claus, and all such prowling gentlemen."

Nevertheless, Emily rebelled when Miss Lyon announced the girls were to remain in their rooms and meditate to order. If the school was in favor of this plan, Miss Lyon directed, the school would rise. Everyone stood up but Emily and her roommate. Greatly shocked, Miss Lyon went on to say that if anyone was so "lost to a sense of the meaning" of Christmas and wished to spend it otherwise, she should rise. Emily alone rose. She was given permission to take the afternoon stage to Amherst, thereby causing quite a disturbance in her family circle. No life of hers tells us how her insurrection was explained, but she was permitted to return to the Seminary unrepentant and still of the same mind. Possibly the matter of her health was given as an excuse.

Emily was happy to go home again for recess between January 20 and February 4, 1848. On her return to school she wrote Austin that she thought of home and the "cheerful meal" and the "merry laugh," and her chair empty. She counted the weeks—twenty-two, and "home again"—until she could leave her boarding school for her *dear dear* home," just as her mother had counted them a quarter of a century before.

February came and St. Valentine's Day. Miss Lyon forbade the sending or receiving of "those foolish notes called valentines" under penalty of punishment, possibly because of their Popish association. But the village postmaster had been approached earlier, had taken the girls' part, and some 150 valentines were sent, though Emily did not write one. She complained to Austin plaintively that all the week before February 14 she had looked in vain, "pining for a valentine," and had not yet given up hope. After mentioning the fun at home in Amherst the previous year at Valentine time, she added that she supposed Vinnie had received "scores" while she, the *"highly accomplished & gifted elder sister,"* was ignored.

Emily, with her high gift of intelligence, could not have failed to notice how much the prettier of the two Vinnie was. In fact, she wrote that Vinnie must "look her prettiest" when she came to visit at Mount Holyoke, to live up to the "glowing account" Emily had given of her. Vinnie was a great mimic, lots of fun, and considered not a little "vain." Emily was not without her own innocent vanity, but she may have been writing with tongue in cheek when she said, in one of her earlier letters, "I am growing handsome. I expect I shall be the belle of Amherst when I reach my seventeenth year. I don't doubt but that I shall have perfect crowds of admirers at that age,—but away with my nonsense." At any rate, the two sisters loved each other dearly all of their lives.

It seems likely to suppose that Emily, being a teen-age girl, worried over something that causes concern to all teen-age girls—her figure. At fourteen she wrote to Abiah about her changing appearance and the fact that she was growing older. She added: "But my"—and the next word is missing in her published letter—"has not changed, nor will it in time to come. I shall always remain the same old sixpence." Looking at Emily's picture, taken when she was seventeen, one sees that she had cause to worry, for she was still sadly lacking in curves.

By March Emily had developed a racking cough, which was reported to her family by a visitor from Amherst who thought she was looking very ill. Mr. Dickinson, badly frightened, sent Austin to bring her home at once. She fought and pleaded with him and even shed tears, for her wish was to complete the term. But she was ignominiously bundled up, driven home, and put to bed. A letter to 'Biah describes her state:

> . . . Austin arrived in full sail, with orders from head-quarters to bring me home at all events. . . . Austin was victorious, and poor, defeated I was led off in triumph. . . . I could not bear to . . . go home to be dosed . . . and be condoled with on the state of health in general by all the old ladies in town.
>
> Haven't I given a ludicrous account of going home sick from boarding-school? Father is quite a hand to give medicine, especially if it is not desirable to the patient, and I was dosed for about a month after my return home, without any mercy, till at last out of mere pity my cough went away. . . . Father has decided not to send me to Holyoke another year, so this is my *last term*. . . . Father wishes to have me at home a year, and then he will probably send me away again, where I know not.

But Father never did. Instead he decided that she should remain at home the following year, taking some classes at Amherst Academy, which she did, much to the delight of friends and classmates, for she was the wit of the school and her compositions sent them all, including the teachers, into gales of laughter.

First she finished the term at Mount Holyoke, however. She had kept up her studies during the months at home, so that when she returned to the Seminary in May she was not behind her class. Still, her thoughts turned to home. She requested permission to go to Amherst for a weekend, but permission was denied. It was against one of the school rules. She tried to console herself again by counting the weeks remaining until she left Mount Holyoke—which the Amherst College boys called the "Fem Sem" or "Miss Lyon's Missionary Rib Society"—forever.

CHAPTER 3

In Between

Back in familiar Amherst, Emily enjoyed going to parties and being as social as the staid town would allow. She was a madcap on many occasions. One day when the divine month of May was stealing over the countryside, the spring after her return from school, Emily was looking forward to an enchanting stroll in the woods. But the whole Dickinson family was obliged to attend a funeral at a church in Hadley—the funeral of some ancient relative about whom Emily knew nothing.

When the brief ceremony was over, she looked about for a way of escape and spied a favorite cousin, Willie Dickinson, who had come to the funeral in his own buggy with a fast horse. A few pleading whispers in that lively youth's ear and Willie nodded and lifted her in. They were on their way before the other mourners spied them. Emily begged that he take her home by way of Sunderland, which was seven miles in the opposite direction.

So speedy was her cousin's mare that the culprit reached Amherst and the Dickinson house before parents and sister returned. They discovered Emily securely locked in her room. No doubt her parents saw nothing ahead of her but certain doom after such unheard of behavior. Her mother came up, bade her unlock the door, lectured, and wept over her for some time. Her father, who never reproved in words, only by ignoring the sinner, took no notice of his elder daughter at meals for a day or two. She, who knew him so well, saw that he was very angry. Vinnie was, of course, on her sister's side. But, again, the erring one showed no sign of contrition. She had gratefully saluted a perfect May day.

The Dickinsons at that time lived in a house on Pleasant Street. The family mansion had been sold in 1833, although they had continued to reside in one part of it until 1840. It was not until 1855 that the mansion was repurchased and refurbished, and the Dickinsons returned.

Wherever they resided, the Dickinson household was a busy one. The three women had constant household duties to perform, and Mr. Dickinson expected them to be performed well. At one time, when he complained that a nicked plate seemed constantly to be put on the table before him, Emily took it outdoors and smashed it into smithereens so it would not offend him again.

In those days, there were no time-saving household conveniences—all tasks had to be performed by hand. In later years Emily did her reading and writing at night because there was no time for anything but housework during the daylight hours. Lines from one of her poems attest to this:

> Unto my books so good to turn
> Far ends of tired days.

Although Edward Dickinson advertised for a hired girl in 1850, no one suitable was found at the time. Furthermore, a constant procession of guests came to the Dickinson household, and none was ever turned away. Before 1853 they came by private carriage or by the stagecoach which also carried the mail. So, besides the scrubbing and the dusting, the cooking and the baking, the washing and the ironing, the sewing and the knitting, the three Dickinson women had to be prepared to entertain at a moment's notice and for as long as the guests chose to stay. Tired of a relative who said he'd stay a month if it weren't for his business, Emily remarked that it was fortunate for the Dickinsons that his business felt the need of him.

When Emily returned from Mount Holyoke Seminary, both Austin and Lavinia were at home, so for a while there was no need to write letters to one another. But in the fall of 1849, when she was sixteen, Lavinia's turn came to go away to school. With Jane Hitchcock, the daughter of Edward Hitchcock, then president of Amherst College, for a roommate, Vinnie traveled over one hundred miles to Ipswich Female Seminary. Both girls wrote to Austin—Vinnie must have felt herself inferior to her brilliant sister and brother for she begged Austin not to "ridicule" her letters. Jane painted a rather dismal picture of Ipswich in a letter to Austin—the students were constantly exhorted to "restrain" their feelings and *"put on the screws"* in their studies, because they were not at school or in life to *"have a good time."* Jane wrote that she would be "crushed" by all this if it were not for Vinnie, who could "take off" people and provide a "good laugh." She told Austin, "Vinnie writes all the funny letters that go from this room."

[17]

Both girls stated that they felt slighted by all the good times going on at Amherst, as if to celebrate their departure. Vinnie lamented that Amherst was "never so gay, before," saying that Emily had written of a *"grand"* sleigh ride.

Emily, in January of 1850, did indeed describe a sleigh ride "on a very magnificent plan" to her friend and former classmate, Jane Humphrey. A party of ten from Amherst met another party of ten and had a "frolic" which included music, charades, conversation, and supper. She did not tell if Mr. Dickinson was pacing the floor when she and Austin reached home at two in the morning, but said they were not the worse for wear because of the late hour.

Vinnie apparently was at home for another frolic, when the P.O.M. meeting was held at the Dickinson house. Emily Fowler, Emily Dickinson's friend since childhood, conceived the brilliant idea of the "Poetry of Motion" meetings. Dancing was frowned upon in Amherst—but the young people yearned to dance. The parents did not seem to know what their young people were doing at the P.O.M. meetings as they lumbered about to the tune of the piano. The secrecy made the fun even sharper. And when Mr. and Mrs. Dickinson planned an overnight stay away from home, Emily and Austin grew so bold as to hold a P.O.M. meeting in *their* house. Unfortunately for them, when they replaced a lion rug they had rolled up for the dancing, they did not notice it was upside down! Mrs. Dickinson, on her return the next day, discovered it and was horrified to learn the reason. But after some consideration, and at the urging of the girls, she decided not to "trouble" Father with the matter.

But the elders of Amherst were troubled, and Father with them. A religious renewal—known as the Great Revival—was sweeping New England in 1850. This increased spiritual awareness worked like a leaven, bringing people to declare themselves for Christ. The feeling was heightened in Amherst by the sudden and unexpected death in February, 1850, of a 39-year-old professor at the college from scarlet fever.

It seemed that eternity was nearer than they had thought. An undergraduate recalled an "awful stillness" in the halls and called it a scene of "thrilling interest." The lighthearted fun seems to have given way to solemn questioning.

By March, the town voted to close the "rum places" so that the college students would not be "ruined." Mr. Dickinson was in favor of the temperance pledge, and eventually he himself "joined" the church. He had attended the Congregational meetings all his life, but had never formally expressed his conviction. A shy man, he, like Emily, was probably embarrassed at the thought of publicly taking "all the clothes off" his soul. But join the church he did, on August 11, 1850.

Lavinia, too, was caught up in the frenzy of religious awareness. She spent the spring recess of 1850 at home, and on her return to Ipswich she wrote to Austin, "You didn't like me very well, when I was at home," and went on to exhort him to turn to religion. If she had spoken to him often in the same vein during the spring recess, it's understandable that Austin grew a little annoyed! He did not, in fact, embrace the Church until 1856. But Vinnie did, and she fretted over her sister.

Emily resisted. She could not accept all the tenets of the Congregationalist faith and therefore could not stand up and be counted, any more than she could at Mount Holyoke. But she agonized within herself that she continued one of the "lingering *bad* ones." In 1854, when she was almost twenty-four, she wrote: "The minister to-day . . . preached about death and judgment, and what would become of those, meaning Austin and me, who behaved improperly—and somehow the sermon scared me."

Indeed, the doctrines of foreordination and eternal punishment were enough to frighten a strong man, much less someone as sensitive as Emily. She worried about death all through her life, her poetry and letters reflecting her concern with the hereafter: "That bareheaded life—under the grass—worries one like a wasp." But she did write to Abiah in January of 1850 that she felt God was in her room, "looking into" her soul and seeing that she tried to be good.

CHAPTER 4

Joy and Sorrow

As FEBRUARY 14 rolled round each year, Emily resolved to do it honor. Though she had been unable to practice the art of writing valentines at the Seminary, she was capable of producing very high flown ones. One, in particular, was addressed in 1852 to a certain William Howland of Springfield. This inimitable valentine is one of the most utterly exuberant of Emily's flights of mirth and nonsense:

> *Sic transit gloria mundi,*
> How doth the busy bee—
> *Dum vivimus vivamus,*
> I stay mine enemy.
>
> Oh, *veni, vidi, vici,*
> Oh, *caput, cap-a-pie,*
> And oh, *memento mori*
> When I am far from thee.
>
> Hurrah for Peter Parley,
> Hurrah for Daniel Boone,
> Three cheers, sir, for the gentlemen
> Who first observed the moon.

Peter put up the sunshine,
Pattie arrange the stars,
Tell Luna tea is waiting,
And call your brother Mars.

Put down the apple, Adam,
And come away with me;
So shall thou have a pippin
From off my father's tree.

I climb the hill of science,
I "view the landscape o'er,"
Such transcendental prospect
I ne'er beheld before.

Unto the Legislature
My country bids me go.
I'll take my india-rubbers,
In case the wind should blow.

During my education,
It was announced to me
That gravitation, stumbling,
Fell from an apple-tree.

The earth upon its axis
Was once supposed to turn,
By way of a gymnastic
In honor to the sun.

It was the brave Columbus,
A-sailing on the tide,
Who notified the nations
Of where I would reside.

Mortality is fatal,
Gentility is fine,

Rascality heroic,
Insolvency sublime.

Our fathers being weary
Lay down on Bunker Hill,
And though full many a morning,
Yet they are sleeping still.

The trumpet, sir, shall wake them,
In dream I see them rise,
Each with a solemn musket
A-marching to the skies.

A coward will remain, sir,
Until the fight is done,
But an immortal hero
Will take his hat and run.

Good-by, sir, I am going—
My country calleth me.
Allow me, sir, at parting
To wipe my weeping e'e.

In token of our friendship
Accept this *Bonnie Doon*,
And when the hand that plucked it
Has passed beyond the moon,

The memory of my ashes
Will consolation be.
Then farewell, Tuscarora,
And farewell, sir, to thee.

William Howland remains an enigma. He was one of the
young men in Mr. Dickinson's law office. This we know, that
he was so delighted with his valentine (guessing, of course,

who sent it) that he submitted it to the *Springfield Republican*, that sheet so carefully perused by all the Dickinsons. In glancing at the paper, Emily was appalled to discover it and took great pains to conceal it from her stately father.

Young and charming men were beginning to call at the Dickinsons. Emily enjoyed her admirers but never took them very seriously. The time was not ripe. She took an interest in her clothes, speaking of new ones in which she would appear "like an embarrassed peacock." The Dickinsons continued to have many visitors, rich and poor, high and low, for this was the period in which people were "given to hospitality." But Emily resented having her writing and study time interrupted, although it was fun going out to parties.

Sometimes she saw Leonard Humphrey and had a chat with him, noticing how feebly he walked for a young man still in his twenties. Then, at the end of the year 1850, Emily suffered her first real sorrow. Humphrey died suddenly. His passing was a great blow to Amherst College and a shock to the town in general. A letter Emily wrote in January of 1851 to Abiah expresses her sadness:

I write A. tonight, because it is cool and quiet, and . . . I am feeling lonely; some of my friends are gone, and some of my friends are sleeping—sleeping the churchyard sleep—the hour of evening is sad—it was once my study hour—my master has gone to rest, and the open leaf of the book, and the scholar at school *alone,* make the tears come, and I cannot brush them away; I would not if I could, for they are the only tribute I can pay the departed Humphrey.

You have stood by the grave before: I have walked there sweet summer evenings and read the names on the stones, and wondered who would come and give me the same memorial; but I never have laid my friends there, and forgot that they too must die; this is my first affliction, and indeed 't is hard to bear it. . . . when the unreconciled spirit has nothing left but God, that spirit is lone indeed. I don't think there will be any sunshine, or any singing-birds in the spring that's coming. . . . I wish I were somebody else—I would pray the prayer of the "Pharisee," but I am a poor little "Publican."

Emily passed many sad days. Months later a diversion came her way. All the Dickinsons but Austin, who was teaching in a boys' school in Boston during 1851, went to hear the much-talked-of Jenny Lind, who was singing in Northampton. They had barely started when a kicking horse delayed the journey. In an amusing letter to Austin, who had already heard Jenny Lind, Emily wrote of the trials of the trip and of Jenny herself, a touching figure standing alone upon the stage:

. . . I wanted to write you Friday, the night of Jenny Lind, but reaching home past midnight, and my room sometime after, encountering several perils starting and on the way, among which a kicking horse, an inexperienced driver, and a number of Jove's thunderbolts, and a very terrible rain, are worthy to have record. All of us went—just four—add an absent individual and that will make full five. The concert commenced at eight, but knowing the world was *hollow* we thought we'd start at six, and come up with everybody that meant to come up with us; we had proceeded some steps when one of the beasts showed symptoms; and just by the blacksmith's shop exercises commenced, consisting of kicking and plunging on the part of the horse, and whips and moral suasion from the gentleman who drove—the horse refused to proceed, and your respected family with much chagrin dismounted, advanced to the hotel, and for a season halted; another horse procured, we were politely invited to take our seats, and proceed, which we refused to do till the animal was warranted. About half through our journey thunder was said to be heard, and a suspicious cloud came travelling up the sky. What words express our horror when rain began to fall, in drops, sheets, cataracts—what fancy conceive of drippings and of drenchings which we met on the way; how the stage and its mourning captives drew up at Warner's Hotel; how all of us alighted, and were conducted in,—how the rain did not abate,—how we walked in silence to the old Edwards (sic) church and took our seats in the same—how Jennie came out like a child and sang and sang again—how bouquets fell in showers, and the roof was rent with applause—how it thundered outside, and inside with the thunder of God and of men—judge ye which was the loudest; how we all loved Jenny Lind, but not accustomed oft to her manner of singing didn't fancy *that* so well as we did *her*. No doubt it was very fine, but take some notes from her *Echo*, the bird sounds from the *Bird Song*, and some of her curious trills, and I'd rather have a Yankee.

Herself and not her music was what we seemed to love—she has an air of exile in her mild blue eyes, and a something sweet and touching in her native accent which charms her many friends. *Give me my thatched cottage* as she sang she grew so earnest she seemed half lost in song, and for a transient time I fancied she *had* found it and would be seen "na mair;" and then her foreign accent made her again a wanderer—we will talk about her sometime when you come. Father sat all the evening looking *mad*, and yet so much amused you would have *died* a-laughing—when the performers bowed, he said "Good evening, Sir,"—and when they retired "very well, that will do." . . . It wasn't sarcasm exactly, nor it wasn't disdain, it was infinitely funnier than either of those virtues, as if old Abraham had come to see the show, and thought it was all very well, but a little excess of *monkey*!

Emily occasionally practiced verse in her room with the aid of her dictionary but showed these efforts to no one, not even to her devoted Vinnie. One day her father introduced her to a stranger, a young man of twenty-seven whose name was Newton—Benjamin Franklin Newton. He had come to study law in Mr. Dickinson's office in the fall of 1847 when Emily was away at school. He and Emily discovered after several meetings that they were congenial and they often took walks in the woods to find rare flowers and discuss books. Emily always knew the especially rare ones and even guided him to the orchid swamp. She resolved to show him her verses, written in her delicate, spidery handwriting, which she was later to keep tied in a tight little roll and fastened with green string. He took them home to read and said of them that he knew she had the power to be a poet; that her verse bore out that statement and he was impressed with it. But she must work hard at it.

Emily was greatly encouraged and pleased, and from that day he became virtually her teacher, she his pupil. But this was also her playtime, and she had a host of admirers who were always fascinated by her wit, her red curls, the way in which she shook her head and threw up her hands in the air, and by her eyes, so grave one minute, so impishly teasing the next. She valued, however, both Newton's advice and friendship and suffered a real shock when he told her in 1849 that he was leaving her father's law office to return to his home town of Worcester, Massachusetts, and hoped shortly to be admitted to the bar. But they would write to each other and exchange ideas in that way.

Yet Emily knew it would not be the same. She prized the books he gave her, especially Emerson's *Poems* which her father would have thought radical. Her friend did not enjoy good health and after he left Amherst and she heard he had married a nurse, she supposed it was on account of the consumption that threatened him. Even after he was married, he still wrote to her occasionally. In his last letter he made a remark that puzzled her: "If I live, I will go to Amherst; if I die, I certainly will."

The thought or sight of death always made Emily quite ill. She was literally swept by a spasm when, glancing idly at the *Springfield Republican* one evening in March of 1853, she saw in three short lines the notice of Newton's death. This was what might be termed a body blow, so much had she depended on him for counsel on her verse, which was just taking shape and was to become in time such an integral part of her. For a while she was inconsolable and took no interest in anything. Finally, she decided to write to Newton's Unitarian minister and composed the following letter to the Reverend Edward Everett Hale at Worcester's Church of the Unity:

Pardon the liberty Sir, which a Stranger takes in addressing you, but I think you may be familiar with the last hours of a Friend, and I therefore transgress a courtesy, which in other circumstance, I should seek to observe. I think, Sir, you were the pastor of Mr. B. F. Newton who died some time since in Worcester, and I have often hoped to know if his last hours were cheerful and if he was willing to die. Had I his wife's acquaintance I w'd not trouble you Sir, but I have never met her, and do not know where she resides, nor have I a friend in Worcester who could satisfy my inquiries. You may think my desire strange, Sir, but the Dead was dear to me, and I would love to know that he sleeps peacefully.

Mr. Newton was with my Father two years, before going to Worcester—in pursuing his studies, and was much in our family.

I was then but a child, yet I was old enough to admire the strength, and grace, of an intellect far surpassing my own, and it taught me many lessons, for which I thank it humbly, now that it is gone. Mr Newton became to me a gentle yet grave Preceptor, teaching me what to read, what authors to admire, what was most grand or beautiful in nature, and that sublime lesson, a faith in things unseen, and in a life again, much nobler and much more blessed—

Of all these things he spoke—he taught me of them all earnestly, tenderly, and when he went from us, it was as an elder brother, loved indeed very much, and mourned, and remembered. . . . Please Sir, tell me if he was willing to die, and if you think him at Home. I should love so much to know certainly, that he was today in Heaven. . . .

It was believed by the Congregationalists that, to gain Heaven, one must be willing to die, and Emily had been brought up in that faith. She received a reply from Newton's pastor that gave her some comfort. She felt, too, that because of her lost friend's faith in her powers, she must become a poet and a fine one—one that he might be proud of. That meant work.

CHAPTER 5

Commencement

COMMENCEMENT AT AMHERST was a ponderous affair. It was held in August, when the air could be very warm, with a soft haze on the Pelham Hills. Commencement Day was the peak of four days of festivities. A holiday atmosphere hung over the town, and on the common were tent shows and peddlars' wagons, booths and auctions, and every manner of traveling entertainment. People from Amherst and the neighboring villages strolled about—oldsters, as well as boys and their sweethearts. Ladies from the various church committees hurried to spread long tables under the trees for the "collation," a cold but plentiful repast which would be served at the end of the ceremonies. Alumni crowded the town, as well as dignitaries, friends and relatives of the graduates, and zealous missionaries who told of long sojourns in ill-smelling villages far across the sea.

The academic procession formed up at nine in the morning and proceeded to the church. The Seniors were the center of attention, having run their course faithfully and finished with credit.

On Thursday, August 8, 1850, Austin was graduated from Amherst. George Howland, William's brother, was the salutatorian. The sixth man on the program, Austin's oration was entitled "Elements of our National Literature." It is easy to imagine how Mr. Dickinson's chest swelled with pride, how the Dickinson ladies selected their very best to wear, to do him honor, how Emily chose her best cape jasmine for the occasion, for she liked to fasten a knot of flowers to her dress.

Although Austin was certainly the object of their most intense feelings, another graduate was of interest to Emily. After Austin, there were ten more speakers, and an interval of music.

Then George Gould stepped forward. His subject was "The Relation of Self Reverence to Christ." This college friend of Austin, a tall, loose-jointed six-footer of a young man, was studying for the ministry and had sacrificed nerves and health to achieve a suitable record. He was often at the Dickinson house and Emily loved to flirt with him. It is believed that Emily looked upon George with some favor but that Mr. Dickinson did not, considering him too poor and struggling ever to succeed.

There is a story that George Gould proposed to Emily after his graduation, and that Mr. Dickinson then forbade him the house. But Vinnie's diary shows that George Gould came visiting in 1851, so the story is not likely. What is likely is that Emily, being an honest person and not seriously in love with George, refused him if he did indeed propose to her that day, after arranging to meet her in a secluded corner of the garden.

In addition to George Gould, Vinnie's diary for the year 1851 mentioned over a dozen young men, many of them

Austin's friends, as callers at the Dickinson home, including Elbridge Bowdoin, John Emerson, Tutor Edwards, Henry Root, John Sanford, Salter Storrs, George and William Howland, and cousin William (Willie) Dickinson. A young man in whom Vinnie was much interested, Joseph Lyman, also came to call, but he departed from Amherst and eventually married a Southern girl, leaving Vinnie embittered.

Although Commencement Day itself was the highlight of the week for most, to the Dickinsons there was a more important event. On the Wednesday of Commencement Week, Mr. Dickinson held, each year, a reception. Chairs and settees were arranged on the lawn; house and grounds were thrown open to the graduates, guests, and celebrities from six to eight. And the celebrities did come. Mr. Dickinson was a highly thought of citizen, as well as being the treasurer of Amherst College. Even the governor had been known to attend, his staff in uniform with clanking spurs.

Every guest tasted the best their host had to offer. The silver tea service was set out in the stately dining room, and marvelous dishes, both hot and cold, were handed around, with rolls, and syllabub and many varieties of frosted cakes, which were Emily's specialty. A letter survives from Emily thanking Sue Gilbert, after she became her sister-in-law, for the bread Emily had borrowed—and lamenting that, in an abundance of enthusiasm, she had sliced far too much.

Emily always appeared at her father's receptions, even in later years when she was becoming less and less social and more and more of a recluse. Always she was sought out—Annie Howe, the Hollands' daughter, described a commencement reception she attended in her youth. She had not been able to talk to Emily at all because the poet was so "surrounded" by other guests. Emily herself wrote to Mrs. Holland in 1866 that she awaited Commencement with "merry resignation."

But, at Austin's graduation, Emily was still young, still social, still looking forward to marriage, as her letters reveal —she wondered in one to Austin how their father would get on when they all left home. As it turned out, the girls never left, and Austin escaped only to the other side of the "hedge." No record remains to tell us just how far Mr. Dickinson was responsible, but the hints are there throughout the surviving letters.

In 1851 and 1852 Austin was writing to Sue Gilbert's sister Martha, and Emily's letters to him convey love from Mattie, as she was called. But Mr. Dickinson (if Emily is to be believed) favored Sue, and Emily herself idolized her. By June of 1853, Austin was courting Sue, and they became engaged at Thanksgiving. Sue wrote to her brother in Michigan that he would find nothing to object to in Austin, who would "take care" of her. Sue and Austin eventually were married in 1856.

All the young men who came buzzing around Emily and Vinnie went away empty handed. And over the years, many came. In the early fifties, John L. Graves was very dear to Emily. A first cousin of Mr. Dickinson, he often was at the Dickinson house, sometimes staying there as "protection" when Mr. Dickinson and Austin were away. He was romantically handsome, with dark curls and ardent eyes.

"Cousin John's" friend, Henry Vaughan Emmons, though two years younger than Emily, was another favored visitor. Like Ben Newton, Emmons was interested in things literary, and Emily showed him her poems. In 1852 she wrote to Austin that she had gone riding the evening before with *"Sophomore Emmons,* alone," and it was probably he she referred to as a "beautiful new friend." In 1854, she was still going riding with him, even though he was engaged to someone else at that time.

CHAPTER 6

The Railroad

E DWARD DICKINSON was a highly public-spirited man devoted
to the interests of his community. The principal one in the
early fifties was a railroad calculated to speed up travel
throughout the state and countryside.

In May of 1851 he announced to his family that the General Court of Massachusetts had passed an act incorporating
Edward Hitchcock, Ithamar Conkey, Myron Lawrence of
Belchertown, Luke Sweetser, and himself as the Amherst and
Belchertown Rail Road Company. They were to locate, con-
struct, and maintain a railroad by the most convenient north-
erly route through Amherst and neighboring towns. This had
to be completed within four years, but the work could not
even start until all stock for the road had been responsibly
subscribed for and twenty per cent of every share had been
paid into the company treasury.

Of course, Edward Dickinson meant to expend a large sum
out of his own pocket on this worthy enterprise. In February
of 1852 he was able to tell his wife and daughters that the
fifty thousand dollars needed for the Amherst and Belcher-

town railroad had been fully subscribed. He wrote to Austin, who was teaching in Boston, that the railroad was a "fixed fact." Ground was to be broken almost at once.

Mr. Dickinson experienced intense satisfaction in the days that followed. What pride he felt in hearing his fellow townsmen remark, "Well, Dickinson, you did it, you did it at last," and in having a cannon fired off, with people cheering in the streets. The great disappointment in the Dickinson household was that Austin was not home for all the excitement; Emily wrote that she missed his "big Hurrahs" and the "famous stirs" he made on such occasions. She described events to him thus:

> . . . Since we have written you, the grand railroad decision is made, and there is great rejoicing throughout this town and the neighboring; that is, Sunderland, Montague, and Belchertown. Everybody is wide awake, everything is stirring, the streets are full of people talking cheeringly, and you should really be here to partake of the jubilee. The event was celebrated by D. Warner and cannon; and the silent satisfaction in the hearts of all is its crowning attestation.
>
> Father is really sober from excessive satisfaction, and bears his honors with a most becoming air. Nobody believes it yet, it seems like a fairy tale, a most miraculous event in the lives of us all.

And she went on to say they would probably all "fall down and worship the first 'son of Erin' " who came. The Irish put up their "shantees" in Logtown while they built the road. Later, the Dickinsons were to have great affection for the Irish who worked for them.

In the spring of 1853, freight began to move over the new

line, and the first passenger train ran on May 9. Nineteen guns were fired off to celebrate its arrival. The Amherst and Belchertown railway was nineteen and a half miles long and connected with the main line for Boston. Mr. Dickinson wrote jubilantly to Austin, who was then at the Harvard Law School in Cambridge, that the cars would leave at ten minutes after one that day and reach Boston at six. But he added there would be "no railroad jubilee till we see whether all moves right," and then they would "glorify becomingly."

All moved well and, in June, Amherst had its celebration. Emily called it the "New London day" and three hundred guests from that town came on the cars.

Three hundred guests besides all the townsfolk! Emily, who was made ill by crowds, had announced that she could not go to the celebration, though her family was sorely disappointed. They set off in state to attend the great event. In good time, in spite of the heat, Emily left the house and took refuge in the nearby woods where, quite unseen, she could view the train of cars dutifully following its leader, the locomotive, which was breathing out fire and smoke like a dragon. The train rushed around the bend, tore down the track, and was gone before any observer could explain or cheer. Later she was to write:

> I like to see it lap the miles,
> And lick the valleys up,
> And stop to feed itself at tanks,
> And then, prodigious, step
> Around a pile of mountains. . . .

She said in a letter to Austin, "While I write, the whistle is playing, and the cars just coming in. It gives us all new life, every time it plays." And, to Austin, she described the activities of June 9, 1853:

> The New London day passed off grandly, so all the people said. It was pretty hot and dusty, but nobody cared for that. Father was, as usual, chief marshal of the day, and went marching around with New London at his heels like some old Roman general upon a triumph day. Mrs. H. got a capital dinner, and was very much praised. Carriages flew like sparks, hither and thither and yon, and they all said 't was fine. I "spose" it was. I sat in Professor Tyler's woods and saw the train move off, and then came home again for fear somebody would see me, or ask me how I did. Dr Holland was here, and called to see us—was very pleasant indeed, inquired for you, and asked mother if Vinnie and I might come and see them in Springfield.

A month later, Dr. Holland came to the Dickinsons again, and brought his wife. Emily wrote her brother that the visitors came unexpectedly but they all had a "charming" time, with champagne, presumably opened by Mr. Dickinson, for dinner. Emily and Vinnie promised that they would visit the Josiah Hollands after Commencement.

CHAPTER 7

Visit to the Hollands

THE PROMISED VISIT to the Hollands was accomplished in September of 1853. The nine o'clock train on the new railroad deposited the sisters three hours later at the Springfield station, where tall, dark Dr. Holland met them. His wife was waiting at the Holland cottage, only a short drive away by carriage. With the sweet, blue-eyed Elizabeth Holland was her small daughter Annie, and her then unmarried sister, Minnie Chapin.

The Dickinson girls enjoyed their visit with the Hollands very much. So much, in fact, that they repeated it the following fall, presumably to attend the Springfield flower show. We surmise the Dickinson sisters appreciated the relaxed atmosphere of the Holland home, the love so evident there—and the joy, so different from the more rigid atmosphere of the house on Pleasant Street. Emily mentioned that she loved the way the lamps shone on the Hollands' "evening table."

For Mr. Dickinson was a strict disciplinarian. As much as Emily loved and respected him, she must have had the same difficulties with him that nearly every teen-age girl experiences with her father. In 1852 she wrote to Austin describing an evening when Mr. Dickinson, who had been ill, was ensconced in the sitting room. Some young men came calling and Emily miserably "endeavored to *make conversation*" in the awkward situation until some relatives luckily arrived. Mr. Dickinson and his guests finally adjourned to the kitchen fire, leaving the young people to enjoy the evening.

A year earlier she had intimated in another letter to Austin that their father was stubbornly set in his ways, saying that his mind was "formed"—or, in modern parlance, that he was a square.

Another time (in May of 1853), Emily wrote Austin about the visit of some relatives. Apparently she had to listen while they agreed with her father on the "present generation," and hoped that "every young man who smoked would take fire." When Emily voiced her opinion, she stated that she was "instantly put down"—perhaps the first such "put down" on record.

She complained to Austin once that their father's real life and hers did not agree and, in 1852, that "Mother has been sick . . . & Father 'is as he is,'" so that home was a gloomy place. Vinnie, too, made complaints, writing to Austin, "Eyes has he but he will not see."

So the warmth and informality of the house in Springfield must have been a revelation to Emily. Years later she wrote to Mrs. Holland that she would never forget the Doctor's prayer that first morning of their visit, because it was "so simple, so believing. *That* God must be a friend—*that* was a different God—and I almost felt warmer myself, in the midst of a tie so sunshiny."

Both Emily and Vinnie thought the Hollands were "charming and good," not sophisticated or worldly. Emily

was fond of Minnie, too, including her in her letters, refer-
ring happily to the "dumb-bells" Minnie had used during
one of their visits.

Emily remained friends with Elizabeth Holland all her
life, and wrote her many letters. Mrs. Holland was a good
housekeeper and a thrifty person, even working on her husband's overcoat. But her sewing and mending, along with all
the other housewifely chores, did not impede the use of her
quick mind and wit, or her joy in life.

The "birdlike" Mrs. Holland, born Elizabeth Chapin, and
the Doctor were married on October 7, 1845. He had been
practicing medicine in Springfield but found his struggles
futile, while he was drawn more and more to a literary life. He
founded a newspaper which died in six months, and when he
and his wife removed to Vicksburg on the Mississippi, he or-
ganized the school system there. Summoned back to Springfield in the spring of 1849 by family illness, he was looking
desperately for work when he happened to pass the daily *Republican* office and saw Samuel Bowles, the envied editor,
standing in the doorway. Dr. Holland realized that this was
the place he wanted to be. He had sent his "Sketches of Plan-
tation Life" to the paper while in the South but he had small
hope of obtaining a position there.

Samuel Bowles recognized him and apparently thought
that he could use a literary assistant to write book reviews
and start a religious and ethical department. When they met
to discuss the matter, Holland concluded that he could work
with Bowles, despite their differences in religion. He was
given the job of associate editor to Bowles. Samuel Bowles
was also a great friend of Austin Dickinson. He was to become a very important force in Emily's life.

CHAPTER 8

Two Portentous Visits

IN DECEMBER OF 1853, some months after the first visit to the Hollands, Mr. Dickinson was called to Washington for two years while Congress was in session. Edward Dickinson did not go to the Thirty-third Congress from motives of personal ambition but to further a special cause in which he was vitally interested—freedom. As a member of the House of Representatives, he was expressing his liberal views against the passage of the Kansas-Nebraska Bill. Forty-four Northern Whigs, of whom he was one, had been fighting this bill of Stephen A. Douglas with all their might. The bill had again made the slavery dispute an open wound between North and South.

What was happening to his ladies left at home? Vinnie, at least, bemoaned the extra work she had to do, and complained to Austin of how things went when the head of the house was away, even though she appeared to enjoy the freedom from his rule. She also mentioned to her brother that their father did not seem to be very happy about his enforced absence from home.

However, Mr. Dickinson traveled back to Amherst several times during the winter and spring of 1853–1854, as did Austin, who was at the Harvard Law School. One of Austin's visits was to attend the wedding of Emily Fowler and Gordon Lester Ford.

March found Mrs. Dickinson and Vinnie in a bustle of preparation. The village seamstress was spending days in the house, cutting and fitting gowns both old and new. Many packages and boxes had been arriving from Boston stores. Hats and bonnets and fashionable mantles appeared, and new gowns whose skirts were like bells—evening frocks of filmy stuff, gauze and illusion, with many flounces, cut low in the neck and off the shoulders, and garnished with artificial flowers.

The reason for all this commotion was that Mr. Dickinson, who never did anything by halves, had determined that his wife and daughter should have the pleasure of a visit to the nation's capital at the prettiest time of the year—the spring. He had told them to get what finery was needed for such a state occasion. He had instructed Austin to escort his mother and sister on their way, being aware of his wife's timidity on any journey. Probably realizing that Emily already showed great disinclination to leave her home, he nevertheless wrote instructions to bring "Emily too, if she will."

Emily wouldn't. And, as a result, Vinnie was undecided. She wrote Austin, asking if he thought it best she should go, because she hated to leave Emily at home alone. On March 16, Emily wrote Austin that her mother and Vinnie were preparing for the trip. Emily herself seemed to be busily lining up people to stay with her while they were gone: "Cousin John is going to stay here at night when they are away," she wrote a few days later. Mr. Dickinson advised Austin that his mother and Lavinia were coming to Washington about April 1 but made no mention of Emily.

Poor Austin! It is a wonder that he was able to pass the bar, which he did that spring of 1854, with the demands made on his time by his family. His father even caused him to miss his own graduation in order to accompany his mother on a trip to Monson that she wished to make at just that time. Emily was constantly writing Austin to pick up medicine for her at the chemist's, and Vinnie had him running all over Boston matching samples and buying ribbons. Even his mother once commissioned him to buy her a hat! And both girls peppered him with demands that he write them—constantly and time consumingly. Bound by so many loving strings, it is small wonder that Austin was never really able to escape completely.

For years it was believed that Emily suddenly changed her mind at the last minute and accompanied her mother, Vinnie, and Austin to Washington, making the trip with them in two days and stopping overnight at the Astor House in New York. Certainly Mrs. Dickinson, Vinnie, and Austin went; a contemporary account places them at Willard's Hotel in Washington on April 16, 1854. But a letter Susan Gilbert wrote to a friend tells of staying with Emily—"keeping house with Emily while the family are in Washington" was the way she put it.

Willard's Hotel did have the names of "E. Dickinson and daughters" on its guest list of February 10, 1855. Whether Emily went in 1855 when she wouldn't go in 1854—and why—remains another of the mysteries surrounding her. Perhaps it was so Vinnie could repeat the trip, as it appears that Mrs.

Dickinson remained at home in 1855. For go to Washington Emily obviously did; a contemporary writes of seeing Mr. Dickinson and his "two daughters" at Willard's, but does not give the year. A book inscribed in 1855 was presented to Emily at Washington, and a letter she wrote to Sue instructs her to tell "Mother and Austin" they were not forgotten by the two sisters. She had been away just five weeks, Emily wrote later: "We were three weeks in Washington, while father was there, and have been two in Philadelphia." From one of Sue's letters, it seems that Mr. Dickinson escorted the two girls to Philadelphia to visit the Colemans and then went on home to Amherst himself.

Perhaps Emily went to Washington because she knew it would please her father. Certainly Vinnie had brought back exciting stories of great persons from the 1854 visit. For, in 1854, there was much excitement in the Congress. Stephen A. Douglas' bill which would give to Kansas and Nebraska the right to decide whether they would be slave or free, in spite of the Missouri Compromise, came up for a vote in the Senate on March 3, 1854, and was passed by 37 to 14.

On March 21 the Kansas-Nebraska Bill was introduced in the House, and referred to the Committee of the Whole because of opposition. Mr. Dickinson wrote to Austin that this was probably the end of it. However, eventually the bill did pass, and President Franklin Pierce signed it into law on May 30. Shortly after the bill passed the House, a meeting was held in Mr. Dickinson's rooms at "Crutchett's" at Sixth and D Streets. It was decided, following much discussion, that the only hope of victory for the forces of freedom lay in a new party, for which the name Republican was judged appropriate.

[48]

Emily had always taken an interest in politics. She knew that her father had been a personal friend of "Black Daniel," as they called Daniel Webster, and had helped to nominate him for President. Now her father was on a Congressional Committee to investigate conditions at the armories, one at Springfield, Massachusetts, and one at Harper's Ferry, Virginia. Emily knew that he was acquainted with many of the great and near great in the Nation's capital.

Whatever her reason for going, and whatever the year, Emily's reaction to Washington was one of pleasure. In a letter to the Hollands she speaks of a "pleasant time" and describes a visit to Mount Vernon. She and Vinnie journeyed to the historic spot by gliding "down the Potomac in a painted boat," walked hand in hand along the path to the tomb where they stood in awe, and entered the house. She did not describe for the Hollands their passage through the stately home, but it is easy to imagine the two girls lingering over the magnificent carpet Louis XVI had ordered manufactured especially for George Washington or exclaiming over the Windsor chairs. They must have seen the slave quarters and the gardens and the greenhouse. Emily mentioned the balmy spring weather in her correspondence. If she went in 1855, the month was February. Another mystery—unless she liked Washington so well that she went twice!

Emily was obviously very social in Washington. Her father took her to the Capitol where she could look down from the new wing into the Senate Chamber and see the famous people, many of whom she met. Her constant reading of the newspapers and the talks she had had with older men, her father's friends who lived in or visited Amherst, stood her in good stead now. The Dickinsons went to a big levee at the hotel one afternoon and met Emily's childhood friend, Helen Fiske, on the arm of her soldier husband, Edward Bissell Hunt, whom she proudly presented to the Dickinsons. Helen was beautifully dressed, the gayest of the gay, and her old friend felt quite provincial beside her. From what he had heard from his wife about Emily, Lieutenant Hunt thought her a blue-stocking—but changed his mind. Since Emily did not dance, he sat and talked to her and found her, as he said, "most delightful." The two became friends; she said of him that he interested her more perhaps than "any man she ever saw."

There were those who said, later, that it was Lieutenant Hunt with whom Emily fell in love. This is doubtful. Austin described the officer in a most uncomplimentary fashion, calling him an ambling, long-faced, ungraceful "older man."

One night there was a glittering formal dinner at the Willard Hotel. Cabinet members, diplomats, and one or two generals were present. The Dickinsons were among the invited guests. Emily was soon recognized as having insight into world affairs and as possessing as well a pungent wit and a radiant and unusual presence. The family long remembered the story of her asking a stiff old justice of the Supreme Court who was seated next to her, when a plum pudding blazing in brandy was handed around, "Oh, sir, may one eat of hell fire with impunity here?" And then she and the judge talked together like old friends as they strolled down the hall after dinner. Emily seemed gayer than she had ever been in her life. Hardly a day of the visit passed without an opportunity of stimulating talk with somebody. She had longed to meet Jefferson Davis, the Secretary of War, but when she did see him, thought he had "an icy countenance."

[50]

Emily Dickinson

Edward Dickinson

Emily Norcross Dickinson

Lavinia Dickinson

Austin Dickinson   *Susan Gilbert*

The house on Pleasant Street

John L. Graves

Leonard Humphrey

Abiah Root

George Gould

Thomas Wentworth Higginson

The Dickinson homestead

Dr. Josiah Holland

Elizabeth Chapin Holland

Helen Hunt Jackson

Edward Bissell Hunt

John Langdon Dudley

Otis Lord

Samuel Bowles

Charles Wadsworth

Martha (Mattie) Dickinson   *Edward (Ned) Dickinson*

Thomas Gilbert (Gib) Dickinson

The mystery of Emily deepens. The Washington visit must have proved to her that she could be part of this scene, this brilliant new world. She could fit in, for she found she was able to hold older men in conversation. It must have been a joy to her to find conversationalists on her own level. Previously she had complained to Austin that even he did not comprehend her, and she was yet to write, "All men say 'What' to me, but I thought it a fashion."

Emily, in fact, was capable of being several different Emilys —a proud and worldly Emily, loving parties, liking to gather people around her; or an Emily who was a flirt and kept one man after another guessing, an Emily who eventually would fall passionately in love. Or she could be a withdrawn Emily, a poet watching the world but not part of it. The forces, external and internal, were at work.

When their weeks in Washington were drawing to an end, she wrote to Sue about their proposed visit to her old friend Eliza Coleman: "We think we shall go to Philadelphia next week though Father has not decided. Eliza writes every day and seems impatient to have us. I don't know how long we shall stay there or in New York. Father has not said."

When Mr. Dickinson made up his mind, his now traveled ladies went to Philadelphia with its scrubbed stoops and serene Quaker folk, so different from the languid atmosphere of Washington where no one ever seemed to hurry and there were continual Congressional wranglings. Eliza lived with her father, the Reverend Lyman Coleman, in a large house on Chestnut Street where he conducted the Presbyterian Academy of Philadelphia. Dr. Coleman had had a pastorate at Belchertown for several years and had then moved to Amherst. Handsome and good-natured, he taught the classics and was an able scholar. When Emily was a little girl she had studied German with him because her father wished it.

There must have been much for the girls to talk about, after their long separation. Eliza wanted to hear all the news, including that about Helen Fiske Hunt and her new husband, and about Emily Fowler Ford's wedding. It is highly probable that, on Sunday morning, Emily went with the Colemans to their place of worship, the Arch Street Presbyterian Church, to hear its brilliant preacher, Charles Wadsworth. How else to explain their long correspondence and the fact that the minister visited Emily in Amherst? No scrap of letter remains to testify to this meeting, but researchers concur that it must have taken place, and that Emily must have been impressed with Dr. Wadsworth. The preacher looked faintly Italian with his dark eyes, over which he wore glasses, and his black hair that came down to his collar. It was his presence, however, that was most commanding, and his deep voice. As he spoke, he seemed to be the exponent of a great and lasting spiritual belief. Emily, who was searching her soul for truth, perhaps found relief in hearing this man. There is evidence that she found more than relief. Had the blow struck them both during that momentous visit to Philadelphia?

CHAPTER 9

Crisis

WHEN EMILY RETURNED to Amherst, did she have a new interest in life? Was she doomed by her own heart, as her niece Martha, Austin's daughter, later said she was? Had she met Dr. Wadsworth, that extraordinary and, unfortunately for her, married man in Philadelphia? There's no doubt the two communicated by means of letters. Hers she sent secretly by trusted friends: "I enclose a note, which if you would lift as far as Philadelphia . . . would please me," she wrote to Mrs. Holland, adding a request that the Doctor address it for her. Wadsworth's letters to her were burned after her death, at her request, except for one. It has been reported that he read her letters to him aloud to his family.

Dr. Wadsworth was described by contemporaries as of a cordial and happy disposition, although shy. Emily saw him as a "Man of Sorrow." She never really knew much about him; after his death she wrote to his friends asking what he was like. Perhaps she chose him to love because he was so unattainable—it saved her from even a pretense of trying to break away from home. She could worship him safely, from a great distance.

Emily gave her confidence to no one, not even Vinnie, and continued to perform all her household tasks as usual, though she was animated by a hidden fire. Dr. Wadsworth's portrait hung in her bedroom for the rest of her life, and his letters were hidden in a secret drawer.

A poem about the letters fairly wrote itself:

> Going to him! Happy letter! Tell him—
> Tell him the page I didn't write;
> Tell him I only said the syntax,
> And left the verb and the pronoun out.
> Tell him just how the fingers hurried,
> Then how they waded, slow, slow, slow;
> And then you wished you had eyes in your pages,
> So you could see what moved them so.
>
> Tell him it wasn't a practised writer,
> You guessed, from the way the sentence toiled;
> You could hear the bodice tug, behind you,
> As if it held but the might of a child;
> Almost you pitied it, you, it worked so,
> Tell him—No, you may quibble there,
> For it would split his heart to know it,
> And then you and I were silenter.
>
> Tell him night finished before we finished,
> And the old clock kept neighing "day"!
> And you got sleepy and begged to be ended—
> What could it hinder so, to say?
> Tell him just how she sealed you, cautious,
> But if he asks where you are hid
> Until to-morrow,—happy letter!
> Gesture, coquette, and shake your head!

In the eventful year of 1856, Austin married Sue Gilbert, whom he had been courting for years. He resolved to succeed his father in the law office, and there was no further thought of Chicago where he and Sue had once planned to settle. Mr. Dickinson, proud and delighted, built them a charming house across the lawn—just "a hedge away." Many joyous happenings took place in that house, which was for some years like a second home to Emily. But both her brother and sister-in-law noticed the increasing change in her.

It was in the early fifties that the first hints of one of the mysteries surrounding Emily can be noticed in her letters. She was starting to withdraw into herself—she had refused to go to the celebration on the New London day but sat alone in the woods to watch the train, running home quickly for fear someone would speak to her. On June 19, 1853, she wrote Austin that things were "blue" that day, that she hardly knew what to do because everything looked so strangely. This letter, written just two months after the death of Benjamin Newton, is tainted by sadness. Some think it was the death of a friend—Humphrey, Newton, or the wife of Emily's beloved minister at Amherst—that started her trend toward solitude. Some suggest that it was this minister, the Reverend Edward Strong Dwight, whom she loved, but this does not seem likely.

One day in the early spring of 1860, Emily had a great surprise. Dr. Wadsworth came to call on her, while he was still wearing mourning because of a death in his family. No one knows what Emily thought when she saw this indication that he had suffered the loss of a loved one. Perhaps her heart leaped with the hope that he might be free. Years later she described part of that visit in a letter: " 'Some one has died' I said. 'Yes'—he said, 'his Mother' 'Did you love her,' I asked. He replied with his deep 'Yes.' "

While the minister was visiting Emily, he mentioned his friend James Clark, who lived with his brother Charles in nearby Northampton. No one knows what else the two talked about, but certainly a deep communion passed between them.

Emily's niece tells us that on a day Dr. Wadsworth came, Vinnie (researchers place her in Boston caring for Aunt Lavinia Norcross, who was dying, at the time of his known visit of spring, 1860) ran to Sue with the breathless plea: "Sue, come! That man is here! Father and Mother are away, and I am afraid Emily will go away with him!"

When Vinnie reportedly returned with Sue, the parlor was empty. No sign of any visitor anywhere. No Emily answered their calls. She had gone to her room and locked the door.

Her niece tells us that during the next week Emily did not leave her bed and her heart acted so strangely that the doctor was summoned. He told the family she had had a bad nervous shock which had affected her eyesight and was serious.

Did the minister from Philadelphia make other visits to Emily, as some believe? Possibly in the summer of 1861? Could her niece's description refer to a later visit, when Vinnie was at home and might have run for Sue? Did the minister sit beside Emily in the parlor and explain that he was planning to leave the Arch Street Church and Philadelphia? By the summer of 1861 the Civil War had started, and though he was neither Union or Confederate at heart and his congregation was loyal so far, he felt the time was coming when they would ask for his resignation. For he was neither hot nor cold and the dread struggle of the war was making him restless and affecting his nerves. And so he was accepting a pasturate in California, planning to make the difficult trip across Panama.

The minister was an honorable man, and whether he loved Emily or not, whether he accepted the pulpit so far from her because he did, is not known. But certainly Emily was informed of his impending departure. Perhaps she saw a notice of it in the *Springfield Republican*. Perhaps Dr. Wadsworth wrote to tell her he was thinking of a "removal" long before it became public knowledge. It is more satisfying to suppose that he came to tell her in person.

California, in those days, seemed as far as the moon seems now, or farther. A loved one traveling to the Pacific Coast might never be seen again, it was so long and so dangerous a trip. It was enough of a shock to shatter anyone's nerves.

When less benumbed, Emily sent Sue a copy of the following poem:

Title divine is mine
The Wife without
The Sign.
Acute degree
Conferred on me—
Empress of Calvary.
Royal, all but the
Crown—
Betrothed, without the Swoon
God gives us Women
When two hold
Garnet to garnet,
Gold to gold—
Born—Bridalled—

Shrouded—
In a day
Tri-Victory—
"My Husband"
Women say
Stroking the melody.
Is this the way?

It was during the late fifties and early sixties that Emily found herself as a poet. She had been writing before, but now she was creating hundreds of poems, carefully copying them and filing them away, telling no one of their number. She often wrote little poems and sent them as notes or birthday greetings, but the love poems were more private. She did, however, send a copy of "Title divine" to someone other than Sue—probably Sam Bowles—with a note begging the recipient to "tell no other."

Emily wrote three letters addressed to "Dear Master," copies of which survive. The identity of "Master" has been one of the biggest mysteries surrounding her. The crucial time when Emily appears to have thought that her "Master" loved her in return seems to have been the summer of 1860. Emily was later to write to Mrs. Holland that the month of August had given her the most; April had taken the most from her. It was in April of 1862 that Sam Bowles went to Europe, and Dr. Wadsworth left for California. It was on April 1, 1882, that Dr. Wadsworth died, and "Love has but one Date," she said. She wrote, after his death, that the great friend who offered her solace was gone. She called him "my clergyman," and "my Philadelphia." His faith sustained her, his sermons impressed her. Was he also the man who inspired the poem "I'm Wife"? The mystery lives on, as does the poem:

> I'm wife; I've finished that,
> That other state;
> I'm Czar, I'm woman now:
> It's safer so.
>
> How odd the girl's life looks
> Behind this soft eclipse!
> I think that earth seems so
> To those in heaven now.
>
> This being comfort, then
> That other kind was pain;
> But why compare?
> I'm wife! stop there!

CHAPTER 10

"Mr. Bowles"

AND WHAT OF Samuel Bowles? Some think he was Emily's "Master"; she his "Daisy." She wrote many letters to him and to his wife after 1858, but called him "Master" in none of these. In fact, she referred to him formally as "Mr. Bowles."

Sam Bowles and Austin had met in 1850, and he was the first guest Sue and Austin entertained in their new home across the hedge. So it must have been through Austin that Emily met him. They obviously liked each other immensely, and delighted in each other's brilliance. There were gay evenings at Sue's—Emily later described them as "unnatural," because she felt that bliss was unnatural. A friend who shared them, Kate Scott, said they were "rare." Emily would walk across the path and through the hedge with her big dog to join the fun. These chosen friends who met at Sue's played battledore and shuttlecock. Emily improvised for them upon the piano in her most madcap style, and there was laughter and wit. Once they were caught by Mr. Dickinson, who came lantern in hand across the snow to inquire the meaning of their revels, as it was past midnight. Emily is said to have been so distressed that she ran away from him.

During the early sixties Emily wrote Sam Bowles many letters. And she saw him many times. He was at Amherst for Commencement Week, 1860—that fateful week that many feel was Emily's "day at summer's full."

What happened to her that week? We know of many who came to Amherst for that Commencement. Lou and Fanny Norcross were staying at Sue and Austin's, their mother, Aunt Lavinia, having recently died. The Governor of Massachusetts and his wife were there. Eliza Coleman, back from Philadelphia, was there, with her intended, John Langdon Dudley. Some think it was the Reverend Dudley with whom Emily fell in love, that languid August. She did go to visit Eliza in Middletown in October, and saw John Dudley again. Although Eliza and John were married the following June, members of Eliza's family maintained that John was "Master." But if, as is presently believed, the first of the three love letters to "Master" was written in 1858, this limits the candidates to men Emily had known then.

Both Helen Fiske Hunt and her husband, now a major, were there. Helen reported in a letter that they had "attended church" with the Dickinsons on Sunday and expected to call on them in the evening. We know that Major Hunt met Carlo, said the dog understood gravitation, and thought Emily "uncanny." Of Commencement Week, 1860, Emily wrote to Sue, "Great times."

The Reverend Dwight, who left his congregation at Amherst and moved to Maine a few weeks later, was there. Was "Master" any of these? Or was someone else at that Commencement Week, someone whose name is unrecorded, except in Emily's heart? As noted, at least one researcher feels that Dr. Wadsworth made a summertime visit to Amherst. Could the minister from Philadelphia have been there during that summer of 1860?

Emily was writing her finest love poetry. She felt herself desired and was pouring out her joy in exquisite words—sitting up at night in the silent, darkened house, catching infinity in a few short lines. Did she, during that week, find out the love she thought returned wasn't, or at least, not in the way she wanted?

In her letters to "Master," Emily gives us hints about the identity of the man to whom she was writing—she had sent flowers to him; he probably wore a beard; he was going to a "foreign land"; he had been ill; probably he and Emily and Carlo had walked in the meadows together. The gift of the flowers, of which "Master" inquired the meaning, seems to preclude Wadsworth in far-off Philadelphia, except that, in 1883, we know that Emily sent flowers to Helen Hunt Jackson when she was in the West—pressed flowers! Many people for many years have tried to assemble the clues in these letters to form the man who was "Master," but no one can do it—quite.

Was it Sam Bowles? Austin said later that Emily had loved him "beyond sentimentality." She certainly wrote him letters and poems that can only be interpreted as dealing with love. She referred to herself in much of her poetry as either a lowly "Daisy" or a regal Queen—Sam Bowles dubbed her the "Queen Recluse" one time when she refused to come downstairs and see him. He also sent her a little bat—presumably not alive—a not-so-gentle hint of what he thought of her actions.

When he was ill, she wrote him in early 1862:

> While you are sick, we—are homesick. Do you look out tonight? The moon rides like a girl through a topaz town. I don't think we shall every be merry again—you are ill so long. When did the dark happen?
>
> I skipped a page to-night, because I . . . might have tired you.
>
> *That* page is fullest, though.

But Emily also sent Sam Bowles letters to be forwarded, it seems, to someone else. Would he be "kinder than sometimes —and put the name—on—too," she asked him. Women don't usually send love letters in the care of another lover. Is it possible the poems considered to be written to Bowles were only copies of poems in the enclosed letters, destined for "Master"?

CHAPTER 11

Colonel Thomas Wentworth Higginson

IN 1862, Emily saw an Article, "Letter to a Young Contribu-
tor," by Thomas Wentworth Higginson, in the *Atlantic
Monthly*. The article gave advice to would-be writers. Emily
was impressed by it and also by his article on "The Procession
of the Flowers," sent her by Sue Dickinson. She wrote a short
note to the author, enclosing samples of her poetry. Since she
had had not critic nor adviser since her friend, Ben Newton's
death, she invited him to be her literary critic. Her outward
modesty with regard to her poems was great but it is known
that she never made the slightest change to please him. Her
first note to him, written April 16, 1862, ran as follows:

Mr. Higginson—
    Are you too deeply occupied to say if my verse is alive?
    The mind is so near itself it cannot see distinctly, and I
have none to ask.
    Should you think it breathed, and had you the leisure to
tell me, I should feel quick gratitude.
    If I make the mistake, that you dared to tell me would give
me sincerer honor toward you.

I enclose my name, asking you, if you please, sir, to tell me what is true?

That you will not betray me it is needless to ask, since honor is its own pawn.

Higginson, a well-known man of letters, replied. He was interested in her verse but did not think it publishable. It was too "different" for him, perhaps, too new, for indeed, Emily Dickinson was the forerunner of the modern poets.

Ten days later, on April 26, she wrote to him again:

Thank you for the surgery; it was not so painful as I supposed. I bring you others, since you ask, but they may not differ. When my thought is undressed, I can make the distinction; but when I put them in the gown, they look alike and numb.

You ask me how old I am? I made no verse, but one or two, until this winter, sir. . . . You inquire my books. For poets, I have Keats and Mr. and Mrs. Browning. For prose, Mr. Ruskin, Sir Thomas Browne, and the *Revelations*. I went to school, but, in your manner of the phrase, had no education. When a little girl, I had a friend who taught me Immortality; but venturing too near, himself, he never returned. Soon after, my tutor died, and for several years my lexicon was my only companion. Then I found one more, but he was not contented I be his scholar, so he left the land.

You ask of my companions. Hills, sir, and the sundown, and a dog large as myself that my father bought me. They are better than beings, because they know but do not tell; and the noise in the pool at noon excels my piano.

I have a brother and a sister; my mother does not care for thought, and father, too busy with his briefs to notice what we do. He buys me many books, but begs me not to read them, because he fears they joggle the mind. They are religious, except me, and address an eclipse, every morning, whom they call their "Father."

But I fear my story fatigues you. I would like to learn. Could you tell me how to grow, or is it unconveyed, like melody or witchcraft?

You speak of Mr. Whitman. I never read his book, but was told that it was disgraceful. . . . Two editors of journals came to my father's house this winter, and asked me for my mind, and when I asked them "why" they said I was penurious, and they would use it for the world. . . . I read your chapters in the *Atlantic* and experienced honor for you.

Is this, sir, what you asked me to tell you?

Your friend,
E. Dickinson

After receiving further comment from Higginson about her poetry, she wrote to him on June 8:

Your letter gave no drunkenness, because I tasted rum before. Domingo comes but once; yet I have had few pleasures so deep as your opinion, and if I tried to thank you, my tears would block my tongue.

My dying tutor told me that he would like to live till I had been a poet, but Death was as much of mob as I could master, then. And when, far afterward, a sudden light on orchards, or a new fashion in the wind troubled my attention, I felt a palsy, here, the verses just relieve.

Your second letter surprised me, and for a moment, swung. I had not supposed it. Your first gave no dishonor, because the true are not ashamed. I thanked you for your justice, but could not drop the bells whose jingling cooled my tramp. Perhaps the balm seemed better, because you bled me first. I smile when you suggest that I delay "to publish," that being foreign to my thought as firmament to fin.

If fame belonged to me, I could not escape her; if she did not, the longest day would pass me on the chase, and the approbation of my dog would forsake me then. My barefoot rank is better.

You think my gait "spasmodic." I am in danger, sir. You think me "uncontrolled." I have no tribunal.

Would you have time to be the "friend" you should think I need? I have a little shape: it would not crowd your desk, nor make much racket as the mouse that dents your galleries.

If I might bring you what I do—not so frequent to trouble you—and ask you if I told it clear, 'twould be control to me. The sailor cannot see the north, but knows the needle can. The "hand you stretch me in the dark" I put mine in, and turn away. I have no Saxon now. . . . But, will you be my preceptor, Mr. Higginson?

Colonel Higginson, curious, wrote and asked Emily for a likeness of herself. She replied:

Could you believe me without? I had no portrait, now, but am small, like the wren; and my hair is bold, like the chestnut burr; and my eyes, like the sherry in the glass that the guest leaves. Would this do just as well?

It often alarms father. He says death might occur, and he has moulds of all the rest, but has no mould of me . . . I am happy to be your scholar, and will deserve the kindness I cannot repay.

If you truly consent, I recite now. Will you tell me my fault, frankly, as to yourself, for I had rather wince than die. Men do not call the surgeon to commend the bone, but to set it, sir, and fracture within is more critical. And for this, preceptor, I shall bring you obedience, the blossom from my garden, and every gratitude I know.

Emily constantly begged Higginson to help and advise her in her writing, and she promised to follow that advice but didn't. What she did do in one of her letters of April, 1862, was highlight another mystery: "I had a terror since September, I could tell to none; and so I sing, as the boy does of the burying ground, because I am afraid." What she feared has not been determined, though many feel it was the problem with her eyesight that was worrying her.

There is little doubt that Emily at times annoyed her preceptor. Besides refusing to follow the advice she begged for, some of the letters she wrote him can only be classified as strange. Higginson, who was the colonel of the first Negro regiment during the Civil War, must have been shocked to receive, while in camp in South Carolina in 1863, the following note:

Should you, before this reaches you, experience Immortality, who will inform me of the exchange? Could you, with honor, avoid death, I entreat you, sir. It would bereave
Your Gnome.

Even the most unsuperstitious soldier might well feel a chill at receiving such a communication.

After the war ended, until 1870, their letters were all that Emily and Higginson knew of each other. He invited her to come to Boston to a meeting at which he was to read a paper on the Greek goddesses. But she gracefully declined, saying, "I do not cross my father's ground to any house or town."

So in August of 1870, Colonel Higginson went to Amherst to see her. On August 15 he walked up the main street, having sent word to her that he was coming, and arrived at the white-pillared homestead surrounded by its high hedge. A maid servant took his card and admitted him to the parlor, dark, cool, and "stiffish." Emily lost no time in appearing. A pattering step sounded in the hall and his hostess entered, wearing white piqué and a blue net shawl and carrying two day lilies in her hand, offering them to her guest. She told Colonel Higginson that they were her introduction and apologized for her shyness, explaining that she never saw strangers. But she was anything but shy when they began to talk. "They talked of poetry and puddings, the Bible and Shakespeare, Lydia Maria Child, Longfellow and the Brownings, the joy of living and of her dog Carlo, now dead. He thought as did the majority, that she was plain and said later that her manner reminded him of Bronson Alcott's though hers was more natural and genuine."

He mentions that he saw her twice on that occasion. He must have been persuaded to come back in the evening, but was not asked for tea. He did not meet any other member of the family while in the house, but, while visiting with President William Stearns of Amherst later, spoke of Emily and the Dickinsons. Next morning he met Edward Dickinson before his train left and described him as "dry and speechless." As a parting gift, Emily presented her friend with a picture of Elizabeth Barrett Browning's tomb that had been given to her. He carried away an impression of Emily as "unique and remote." He found her poems "sometimes exasperating, seemingly wayward," but was amazed that a "recluse woman" could grasp "the very crises of physical or mental struggle."

Of all Emily's various men friends, Higginson proved to be the only one who tried to give her what she needed—adequate criticism of her poetry. She sincerely thanked him for his help. In one of her letters she told him he had saved her life and in a sense he had—the life of her mind, in that difficult year, 1862, when both Dr. Wadsworth and Sam Bowles "left the country." It may have been of either Dr. Wadsworth or Sam Bowles that she wrote the following poem:

> I envy seas whereon he rides,
>   I envy spokes of wheels
> Of chariots that him convey,
>   I envy speechless hills
>
> That gaze upon his journey;
>   How easy all can see
> What is forbidden utterly
>   As heaven, unto me!
>
> I envy nests of sparrows
>   That dot his distant eaves,
> The wealthy fly upon his pane,
>   The happy, happy leaves
>
> That just abroad his window
>   Have summer's leave to be,
> The earrings of Pizarro
>   Could not obtain for me.
>
> I envy light that wakes him,
>   And bells that boldly ring
> To tell him it is noon abroad,—
>   Myself his noon could bring,

Yet interdict my blossom
And abrogate my bee,
Lest noon in everlasting night
Drop Gabriel and me.

CHAPTER 12

Boston–and Otis Lord

In 1864, Emily's eyes became so troublesome that she was obliged to go to Boston where, for several months in 1864 and again in 1865, an experienced doctor treated her and cut down mercilessly on her reading and writing. No doubt her father insisted on her having the best advice possible and this was not to be had in Amherst. Her beloved cousins, Louise and Fanny Norcross, were her greatest comfort during these times. It is known that she lived with them at a boarding house in Cambridge, the Hotel Berkely.

In a letter written to Colonel Higginson in the summer of 1864, she sums up her whole situation in her inimitable way. She had not written to him for some time; so had not heard that he had been invalided from the war.

Are you in danger? I did not know that you were hurt. Will you tell me more? Mr. Hawthorne died.

I was ill since September, and since April in Boston for a physician's care. . . . Carlo did not come, because that he would die in jail; and the mountains I could not hold now, so I brought but the gods.

I wish to see you more than before I failed. Will you tell me your health? I am surprised and anxious since receiving your note.

> The only news I know
> Is bulletins all day
> From Immortality.

Can you render my pencil? The physician has taken away my pen. I enclose the address from a letter, lest my figures fail.

Knowledge of your recovery would excel my own.

Earlier she wrote to Vinnie:

. . . It is a very sober thing to keep my summer in strange towns—what, I have not told, but I have found friends in the wilderness. You know Elijah did, and to see the "ravens" mending my stockings would break a heart long hard.

Fanny and Lou are solid gold, and Mrs. B and her daughter very kind, and the doctor enthusiastic about my getting well. I feel no gayness yet—I suppose I had been discouraged so long.

You remember the prisoner of Chillon did not know liberty when it came, and asked to go back to jail. . . . Emily wants to be well—if any one alive wants to get well more, I would let him, first.

It has been suggested that Judge Otis Lord of Salem, her father's friend, who was attending court in Cambridge and was there many months each year, might have come to see Emily, might even have read aloud to her, to help her pass the time. There was a certain sense of humor they shared that Emily called "the Judge Lord brand." Emily's niece reported that once, when she was wearing red-and-white striped stockings, Judge Lord asked her if she was meant to be an advertisement for a tonsorial parlor.

It has further been suggested that Otis Lord was "Master," even though he was old enough to be Emily's father, having been born in 1812. Certainly she loved him in later years and he returned her love. The theme of "royalty" in her poems might have been adopted to fit a man named "Lord."

Otis Lord was graduated from Amherst in 1832, so it is likely that he knew Emily as a baby, and quite possibly held her on his lap. Could his have been the "dizzy" knee to which she once referred? Otis Lord had married—when Emily was only thirteen—a beautiful woman named Elizabeth Farley, with whom he seemed to be supremely happy. They visited often at the Dickinson home, spending at least a week there each year. Is it possible that Emily loved this older man all her life, or did their love develop after Elizabeth Lord died in 1877, on Emily's forty-seventh birthday? She had written to Colonel Higginson in 1876: "Judge Lord was with us a few days since, and told me that the joy we most revere we profane in taking. I wish that was wrong."

A year after Judge Lord's wife died, Emily was writing him: "My lovely Salem smiles at me. . . . I confess that I love him," and in 1880, "It is strange that I miss you at night so much when I was never with you."

It is not known to whom Emily wrote this poem:

> Wild nights! Wild nights!
>   Were I with thee,
> Wild nights should be
> Our luxury!

> Futile the winds
> To a heart in port,—
> Done with the compass,
> Done with the chart.
>
> Rowing in Eden!
> Ah! the sea!
> Might I but moor
> To-night in thee!

The Judge continued his visits to Amherst until he died, bringing his nieces with him. Austin noted on August 23, 1880, that Judge Lord and "Troupe" had arrived at the Amherst House. One of the Judge's nieces referred to Emily as a little "hussy" who was "crazy about men," but Emily's niece pictures tranquil "long hours" spent together by the distinguished jurist and her aunt, who "enjoyed their own adventures in conversation" while the young folk went driving in his carriage.

While Emily could write to her father's old friend most tenderly, asking if he were able to say "Come in" when "his Amherst knocked," she probably brought him up short with the remark, "I dreamed last week that you had died."

In 1884, Otis Lord of Salem did die. Although they never married, they thought of it. The Judge called the tiny Emily "Jumbo," and she wrote him: "Emily 'Jumbo'! Sweetest name, but I know a sweeter—Emily Jumbo Lord."

CHAPTER 13

Ashes of Youth

THOUGH HER FAMILY had been deeply shocked by Emily's sudden collapse early in the sixties and her continuing eye trouble, they never knew the reason for it. Vinnie may have guessed since she did know of Wadsworth's hurried visit. It seems strange that Emily never confided in Vinnie, who was so close to her. We are told that she confided to Sue the story of her life's tragedy, making her swear never to divulge it. Of course, as in any small town, gossip abounded in Amherst, especially after Emily began to put aside all colored dresses and clothe herself in pure white—she seemed to proclaim her love and renunciation with the line "Mine by the right of the white election!" What friends and neighbors thought of the change is not known. They must have accepted this whim as a part of the Emily they knew who had always been "different." Emily herself wrote:

> A solemn thing it was, I said,
>   A woman white to be,
> And wear, if God should count me fit,
>   Her hallowed mystery.

A timid thing to drop a life
   Into the purple well,
Too plummetless that it come back
   Eternity until.

Emily's shattered nerves recovered in time but she was never again the gay, brilliant girl who had captivated Washington. She saw friends and neighbors from time to time but paid fewer and fewer visits and finally took refuge almost entirely in the quiet of her father's house and grounds. She was now past thirty, that fateful age Vinnie once had dreaded so much, and the adventure of living took place inside her in hidden ways. Her father never opposed her slightest wish, though what he might have suspected is not known.

As long as they lived together over the years, her devoted sister took on more and more of the household duties that Emily might be free. When night came, Emily (and often she sat up late, especially in the winter to watch over her flowers and keep them from freezing) was at liberty to read, write, commune with her own ideas, and ponder life in general. "The dead of night and the closed door were to her symbols of release," says her niece. "Emily's own conservatory was like fairyland at all seasons. . . . It opened from the dining-room, a tiny glass room, with white shelves running around it on which were grouped the loveliest ferns, rich purple heliotrope, the yellow jasmine, and one giant Daphne odora . . . and two majestic cape jasmines, exotics kin to her alien soul. . . . A rare scarlet lily, a resurrection calla . . . here it was always summer."

For many years, Emily found her best understanding and comfort in her brother's home across the lawn. She wrote many notes to Sue, and Sue could read between the lines. She must have understood Emily's rebellion as expressed in this poem:

> I'm ceded, I've stopped being theirs;
> The name they dropped upon my face
> With water, in the country church,
> Is finished using now,
> And they can put it with my dolls,
> My childhood, and the string of spools
> I've finished threading too.
>
> Baptized before without the choice,
> But this time consciously, of grace
> Unto supremest name,
> Called to my full, the crescent dropped,
> Existence's whole arc filled up
> With one small diadem.
>
> My second rank, too small the first,
> Crowned, crowing on my father's breast,
> A half unconscious queen;
> But this time, adequate, erect,
> With will to choose or to reject,
> And I choose—just a throne.

Sue certainly understood the renunciation expressed in this:

> There came a day at summer's full
> Entirely for me;
> I thought that such were for the saints,
> Where revelations be.

The sun, as common, went abroad,
The flowers, accustomed, blew,
As if no soul the solstice passed
That maketh all things new.

The time was scarce profaned by speech;
The symbol of a word
Was needless, as at sacrament
The wardrobe of our Lord.

Each was to each the sealed church,
Permitted to commune this time,
Lest we too awkward show
At supper of the Lamb.

The hours slid fast, as hours will,
Clutched tight by greedy hands;
So faces on two decks look back,
Bound to opposing lands.

And so, when all the time had failed,
Without external sound,
Each bound the other's crucifix,
We gave no other bond.

Sufficient troth that we shall rise—
Deposed, at length, the grave—
To that new marriage, justified
Through Calvaries of Love!

All of Emily's burning love had been poured into one cup, and she had seen that cup dashed to the ground and shattered to atoms. Since she had not died then—or rather had died and come back—she could not actually die until the proper moment came.

* * *

The Austin Dickinsons were childless for four years. Then, in 1861, a son was born and named for his grandfather, Edward Dickinson. Her greeting to him and his mother was:

> Is it true, dear Sue?
> Are there Two?
>   I shouldn't like to come
> For fear of joggling Him!
> If you could shut him up
>   In a coffee cup,
> Or tie Him to a pin
> Till I got in,
> Or make Him fast
> To Pussy's fist,
> Hist! Whist!
>   I'd come!

Unfortunately, Ned, as they called him, was always delicate and subject to "attacks," although Martha, born in 1866 and called Mattie, was sturdy. New joy came to Emily with this nephew and niece. To them she was just another child. No treat could be greater than that of being left in her charge while their parents were away. As they grew older she made companions of them and talked to them as equals. They took her entirely for granted and adored her and the tiny notes she sent them.

One Christmas when she had made with her own hands their gift of iced plum cake and candy, she sent it over in the afternoon and with it this note: "Please excuse Santa Claus for calling so early, but gentlemen 1882 years old are a little fearful of the evening air."

Her niece states that no one but their aunt could have

written: "Emily knows a man who drives a coach like a thimble and turns the wheel all day with his heel. His name is Bumble Bee!"

When she sent a little pie to Ned, she sent a little note: "Dear Ned: You know that pie you stole? Well, this is that pie's brother." And when Mattie had a birthday, she sent her a bunch of her best flowers and this greeting: "I am glad it is your birthday. It is this little bouquet's birthday too. Its Father is a very old man by the name of Nature, whom you never saw. Be sure to live in vain, dear. I wish I had."

She gave the children treats from the family larder, anything she could find; and once when she smuggled sweets over to them she sent a note: "Omit to return box. Omit to know you received box." Again she wrote: "The joys of theft are two; first theft; second superiority to detection."

When niece and nephew, perhaps with accompanying friends, gathered under the window of her room, she would let down goodies to them on a long string—maybe her famous caramels! To them, their aunt was always a beloved and mysterious personality.

CHAPTER 14

Change

THE SECOND GREAT BLOW in Emily's life came unexpectedly when she was in her early forties. Of Edward Dickinson's three children, Emily was singularly close to her father and he to her, though the relationship could only be noted by certain very observant friends. To her he represented security, the security of home. She used to say: "When father is asleep on the lounge, the house is full."

Sunday happened to be Mr. Dickinson's favorite day of the week, and it was on a June Sunday in 1874, the fourteenth, that daughter and parent were alone together, as Vinnie and Mrs. Dickinson were resting. They talked quietly and then Emily, sitting at the piano, played the tunes of his favorite hymns, the last being, "Rest from thy loved employ." His pleasure almost embarrassed her. When the afternoon was drawing to a close, he said that he "would like it not to end." When Austin dropped by for a visit, Emily suggested the two men should take a walk together. Next morning when she woke her father for the Boston train, how little she thought that she would not see him again in life.

The next evening, Mrs. Dickinson, Vinnie, and Emily were eating their supper with an empty place at the head of the table. Though Mr. Dickinson had been out of politics for some time, he was again serving on the state legislature and had to be in Boston when it was in session. Suddenly, Austin came in with a piece of paper in his hand, and Emily said to herself, "We are all lost," though she could not tell how. Austin explained that his father had been suddenly taken ill in his quarters at the Tremont House in Boston. His condition was critical, and Austin said he and Vinnie would go immediately, but must drive as the last train had gone. While they hurried their preparations and the horses were being harnessed, a second telegram came with the news of Mr. Dickinson's death.

Emily was in an hysterical condition for a week or more, recalling the time she had spent with him on Sunday. She wandered around the house asking everybody, "Where is he? Emily will find him." Her eight-year-old niece Martha never forgot her aunt's tear-filled eyes and the way her quivering lips kept repeating, "You must remember your grandfather. You must. You must never forget him."

The day of the funeral, on June 19, the mourners were so numerous that the house was filled to overflowing and extra chairs had to be placed outside on the lawn. During the service Emily remained upstairs in her room with her door partly open. She had made a small wreath of white daisies which was the only ornament placed upon the coffin. She wrote to Colonel Higginson of her father's death and said: "His heart was pure and terrible and I think no other like it exists." She told Higginson that Mr. Bowles had been with them; she had spoken to no one else. "I am glad," she wrote, "there is Immortality, but would have tested it my-self, before intrusting him."

Emily may not have witnessed this scene, but her brother, Austin, standing alone beside his father's coffin, bent over and kissed him on the forehead, saying, "I was never allowed to do this in life. I am doing it now."

To her Norcross cousins, Louise and Fanny, Emily later wrote, "Though it is many nights my mind never comes home."

A year to the day of her husband's death, Mrs. Dickinson was stricken with paralysis. Again Emily wrote briefly to her preceptor, "Mother was paralyzed Tuesday, a year from the evening father died. I thought perhaps you would care." She signed it, "Your Scholar."

Emily at last learned to know her mother through those weary months of a long illness, for, though she lived for some time, Mrs. Dickinson became permanently weak and feeble. Emily sat beside her through many days and nights. "I have hardly said 'Good-morning mother,' when I hear myself say-ing, 'Mother, good-night.' She inquires constantly for her husband and why he does not come to see her." Emily dealt with this situation as only she could—and very tenderly. She wrote to the Norcross cousins of her mother's death: "She slipped from our fingers like a flake gathered by the wind, and is now part of the drift called 'the infinite.'" And she added sadly: "We don't know where she is, though so many tell us. . . . I cannot tell how Eternity seems. It sweeps around me like a sea."

CHAPTER 15

Gilbert

IN AUGUST OF 1875, a late child arrived in the Austin Dickinson household and was named Thomas Gilbert for Sue's family. This was shortened to Gib. Austin and Sue had grown apart from each other through the years, and this new son was a much needed link. Healthy, handsome, vivacious, precocious yet mischievous, with a mop of golden hair and his father's blue eyes, he was almost like a being from another world. His brother Ned was fourteen and his sister Martha nine when he put in an appearance. Austin thought hopefully that Gib would carry on the Dickinson line, since Ned was so frail.

The boy shortly became the darling of both households, smoothing over the minor frictions between Vinnie and Sue which had always worried Emily. It was Emily who idolized him from the day he was born, mentioning him always to his mother as "Thy son, our Nephew." He was somewhat less popular with his Aunt Vinnie, because he *would* chase her adored cats. On such occasions he got away with murder:

"Weren't you chasing Pussy?" said Vinnie to Gilbert.

"No, she was chasing herself."

"But wasn't she running pretty fast?"

"Well, some fast and some slow," said the beguiling villain.

Emily sent this chronicle to his mother. Though she was devoted to her sister, Emily was not fond of cats. She added: "Pussy's Nemesis quailed. Talk of hoary reprobates! Your urchin is more antique in wiles than the Egyptian sphinx."

When Gilbert was a child in kindergarten, she sent him "The Bumble Bee's Religion." A dead bee accompanied the poem. "For Gib," said her note, "to carry to his teacher from Emily."

> His little hearse-like figure
> Unto itself a dirge,
> To a delusive lilac
> The vanity divulge
> Of industry and morals
> And every righteous thing,
> For the divine perdition
> Of Idleness and Spring.

Gib and his playmates were permitted to tramp all through Aunt Emily's kitchen, and whatever he wished for, his desire was no doubt granted when she was around.

Alas, why couldn't these happy days go on? For eight years small Gilbert lived in an atmosphere of love and devotion, doing all the natural things boys do. Then, in October of 1883, he was suddenly stricken with typhoid fever and lived only three days. The last night of his life when his family watched beside him, Emily appeared like an apparition from the other house with beautiful flowers in her hand that she laid beside him. Though he was too far gone to show any sign of recognition, he suddenly cried out: "Open the door, the boys are waiting for me."

"Quite used to his commandment," wrote Emily to a friend, "his little aunt obeyed." It was the end.

For many days Emily was too stricken to send any message to her sister-in-law, whose anguish she could fully comprehend. But at last there was a letter very like a poem.

Dear Sue—

The vision of immortal life has been fulfilled. How simply at last the fathom comes! The passenger and not the sea surprises us. Gilbert rejoiced in secrets. His life was panting with them. With what a menace of light he cried, "Don't tell, Aunt Emily." My ascended playmate must instruct me now. Show us, prattling preceptor, but the way to thee! He knew no niggard moment. His life was full of boon. The playthings of the Dervish were not so wild as his. No crescent was this creature—he travelled from the full. Such soar, but never set. I see him in the star and meet his sweet velocity in everything that flies.

> His life was like a bugle
> That winds itself away:
> His elegy an echo,
> His requiem ecstasy.

Dawn and meridian in one, wherefore should he wait, wronged only of night, which he left for us? Pass to thy rendezvous of light pangless except for us who slowly ford the mystery which thou has leapt across!

How could one not imagine that Sue would find consolation in these words! One cannot be sure about Austin. He was completely heartbroken. And Emily, who had lost her parents and her closest friends, was shattered by the breaking of this last golden intimacy.

CHAPTER 16

Letters

NO BIOGRAPHER should attempt a life of Emily Dickinson without paying tribute to the extraordinary quality of her letters. There are none like them, and her correspondence with those close to her, her many friends and acquaintances, was one of her life's greatest pleasures. Many letters burned by her own wish include, alas, Judge Otis Lord's and Helen Hunt Jackson's, as well as Dr. Wadsworth's. But many have been preserved, and many written by her hand survived. Her letters of condolence, often sent to the stricken home with some special flower, are unique. No one knew how to speak to the grieving human heart as Emily did. She used words with such a peculiar felicity of phrase that one wonders whether she always carried this gift with her, pressed close to her heart, even when she first appeared in this world.

To Colonel Higginson she once wrote at the beginning of their friendship:

Dear Friend,—A letter always feels to me like Immortality because it is the mind alone without corporeal friend. Indebted in our talk to attitude and accent, there seems a spectral power in thought that walks alone. I would like to thank you for your great kindness, but never try to lift the words which I cannot hold.

Her whims and wit, her most amusing sides, also found their way into her letters.

In March, 1852, she wrote to her brother Austin in anticipation of a visit:

> How very soon it will be now . . . My heart grows light so fast that I could mount a grasshopper and gallop around the world, and not fatigue him any! The sugar weather holds on, and I do believe it will stay until you come. . . . "Mrs. S." is very feeble; "can't bear allopathic treatment, can't have homœopathic, don't want hydropathic," oh, what a pickle she is in. Shouldn't think she would deign to live, it is so decidedly vulgar! They have not yet concluded where to move—Mrs W. will perhaps obtain board in the celestial city, but I'm sure I can't imagine what will become of the rest.

At her gayest and most wicked, she wrote to the Norcross sisters in 1863: "No one has called so far, but one old lady to look at a house. I directed her to the cemetery to spare expense of moving." And again she proclaimed that "Consider the lilies" was the only commandment she ever kept.

Another time she told Mrs. Holland: " 'House' is being 'cleaned.' I prefer pestilence. That is more classic and less fell."

In a more serious vein, she wrote to Vinnie: "Friday I tasted life. It was a vast morsel. A circus passed the house—still I feel the red in my mind though the drums are out."

And to Mr. Bowles: "My friends are my estate. Forgive me then the avarice to hoard them! . . . Our pastor says we are a 'worm.' How is that reconciled? 'Vain, sinful worm' is possibly of another species. Do you think we shall 'see God'? Think of Abraham strolling with Him in genial promenade!"

After Mr. Bowles' death she wrote his widow:

> I hasten to you, Mary, because no moment must be lost when a heart is breaking, for though it broke so long, each time is newer than the last, if it broke truly. To be willing that I should speak to you was so generous, dear.
>
> Sorrow almost resents love, it is so inflamed.

And again, she wrote Mary Bowles of her late husband: "As he was himself Eden, he is with Eden, for we cannot become what we were not."

Her niece speaks in her *Life and Letters of Emily Dickinson* about her aunt's library: "Although she never went to live in it except in spirit, the world was Emily's real neighborhood. George Eliot's works she called 'that lane to the Indies Columbus was trying to find.' Longfellow, Tennyson, the Brownings, Socrates, Plato, Poe and the Bible sift through her conversation; Keats and Holmes, Ik Marvel, Hawthorne . . . Howells and Emerson, Sir Thomas Browne, De Quincey, George Sand, Lowell—whose 'Winter' enthralled her for days at a time, she declared—and perhaps differently from all the rest the Brontës, all three, Charlotte, Anne and Emily! Shakespeare always and forever, Othello her chosen villain, with Macbeth familiar as the neighbors and Lear driven into exile as vivid as if occurring on the hills before her door." On the walls of her room, beside the picture of Dr. Wadsworth, hung framed portraits of Mrs. Browning, George Eliot, and Carlyle.

CHAPTER 17

One Friend in Particular

Emily was most loyal to her girlhood friends, but there was one special friend with whom as a child she and Vinnie had played under the syringa bushes—Professor Nathan Welby Fiske's daughter, Helen. They attended the same school. Then the Fiskes moved from Amherst. Emily and Helen did not meet for years, though Helen came once or twice to Commencement. Then the Dickinsons heard of her marriage, and found her again during the famous Washington visit.

Helen begged Emily to visit her, and offered to introduce her at a literary salon in New York. Helen Hunt was a child of her age and appeared at this time to have the world at her feet. She had a devoted husband and enjoyed much interesting travel. They had two little sons, but one child died in infancy and, in September of 1863, Major Hunt was killed in an explosion. Helen idolized her second boy, and then he was taken away at nine by "malignant diphtheria." For a time she yielded to despair; but being a brave woman, she took a firm grip on herself and began not only to write but to publish.

When her "Esther Wynn's Love-Letters" appeared under the pen name of Saxe Holm, it was thought she might have had Emily in mind when she wrote it. The same was said of her novel, *Mercy Philbrick's Choice.*

After Helen Hunt moved to Colorado and became deeply fascinated by the Indians, she wrote *Ramona*, her most popular book. She sent the book to Emily, who, though she did not care for it, wrote her most warmly. Meantime, Helen Hunt had remarried. Her second husband was William Jackson, a banker, and by his name she was known to the literary world. She pressed Emily for poems and carried on a determined campaign to persuade her friend to publish. She told Emily that she had a little manuscript volume with a few of her verses in it and that she read them often. She said: "You are a great poet—and it is a wrong to the day you live in, that you will not sing aloud. When you are what men call dead, you will be sorry you were so stingy."

She asked Emily to contribute one poem to the Roberts Brothers' *A Masque of Poets* in the "No Name" series. Emily wrote Colonel Higginson, asking him to advise against it, as an excuse for her. At this stage of her life, Emily seems to have had no desire to see her work published, though she must have thought of it earlier. She had stated that she wished to make Austin and Sue proud of her, and as early as 1851 she wrote to Austin that, while a writer thought little of the value of his line, "eager eyes will search it's every meaning." How truly she spoke! She also wrote to Austin that she had borne one of his letters away to her folio "to amuse nations to come." Yet, all of Austin's letters to her were destroyed at her request at her death.

Helen Hunt Jackson was determined to bring something

of Emily's into print, even if only one poem. Helen knew this book would cause much interest as readers and critics tried to guess the authors of the various poems. On her own, she submitted "Success is Counted Sweetest!" and finally may have obtained Emily's permission, for it appeared in the book, anonymously, like the others. Mrs. Jackson also wished to be appointed as Emily's literary executor. But that wish was never granted, though Vinnie found her letter containing the request, which Emily had ignored in her answer.

When Helen was in the East, she would sometimes drive into Amherst, stop at the Dickinson mansion, and have her horses walked up and down while she enjoyed a talk with her old friend which no member of the family dared interrupt.

The two women continued to correspond. When Helen Hunt Jackson fell and broke her leg in 1884, Emily wrote, "Dear friend, can you walk?" and received the answer, "Dear friend, I can fly!"

"Helen of Troy will die," said Emily, "but Helen of Colorado, never."

Emily felt real loss when Helen Hunt Jackson did die in 1885, only one year before Emily herself bade farewell to the world.

CHAPTER 18

The End of a Poem

IN 1882, the year before Gilbert left them, Emily had a surprise so great that she could never have anticipated it. It was
a summer evening. She heard a visitor being ushered in at
the front door, then a man's voice inquiring for her. Next
came Vinnie's summons: "The gentleman with the deep
voice wants to see you, Emily."

She came flying from her conservatory where she was tend-
ing her lilies and heliotropes, and, like an apparition, Charles
Wadsworth stood before her. She said in glad surprise: "Why
did you not tell me you were coming, so I could have it to
hope for?"

"Because I did not know it myself," he said simply. "I
stepped from my Pulpit to the Train."

"How long has it been?" said Emily breathlessly.

"Twenty years," he answered almost roguishly.

Emily herself described this scene in letters to James and
Charles Clark with whom she initiated a correspondence
after the minister's death. That day, Dr. Wadsworth and
Emily sat down to a long and satisfying talk, the only cloud

being that he remarked casually, "I am liable at any time to die."

He told her of his children—two sons and a married daughter (for he was now 68), but especially of the younger son, Willie, of whom he remarked, said Emily, "The frogs were his little friends." He said Willie reminded him of Emily, not only in appearance but in his love for all small creatures. It was not hard for Emily to tell that he especially cherished his Willie. How she wished she had a picture of the boy. In parting, she said, "The frogs are my dogs," and he smiled at her; and that was the last time she heard the loved voice or saw the face that recollection had kept as it was through the many years of separation.

It was in 1882 that Dr. Wadsworth was suddenly stricken with pneumonia and died swiftly, deeply mourned.

In a letter she wrote to Charles Clark, whose devoted brother had also died after a long illness, Emily said in speaking of her cherished friend Wadsworth: " 'Going home' was he not an Aborigine of the Sky?" And again: "He never spoke of himself and any encroachment I know would have slain him. . . . Heaven might give him Peace, it could not give him Grandeur for that he carried with himself to whatever scene."

In July of 1884, Emily wrote to Louise and Fanny that eight weeks before she had been helping Maggie, their devoted servant, make a cake when she saw "a great darkness coming and knew no more until late at night." She woke to find Vinnie, Austin, and a strange doctor bending over her. For the first time in her life she had fainted and "lain unconscious." She became very ill and alarmed the others, but in time grew better—"am now staying," as she assured them.

Nevertheless, it was the beginning of invalidism, though she lived two years longer.

"Memory's fog is rising," wrote Emily. "It is growing damp and I must go in."

Six months later she wrote the same cousins: "A friend sent me *Called Back*. It is a haunting story, and as loved Mr Bowles used to say, 'greatly impressive to me.'" She still sent occasional penciled notes across the lawn. She wrote Sue: "You must let me go first, Sue, because I live in the sea always now and know the road."

On May 15, 1886, Emily Dickinson passed from the room and home she had so cherished with those she loved best in the world close to her. She was only fifty-six, but serious illness, an advanced case of Bright's disease, had claimed her for many months. The spring she adored was at hand in all its beauty—a tribute to her. A day or two later at the simple funeral in the old house, Colonel Higginson was an honored and welcome guest. How he received the invitation is not known, as he had never met the members of his friend's family with the exception of his brief encounter with Mr. Dickinson. But they all knew how Emily had valued him as her friend and preceptor. Vinnie led him into the room where Emily lay, looking, as he said, "beautiful," with flowers at her throat and in her hand, and an expression of perfect peace on her brow. There was no sign of a wrinkle or a gray hair. While he gazed at her, Vinnie came with two heliotropes which, she whispered to her sister, she was to "take to Judge Lord," as she laid them in the coffin.

Though once a Unitarian minister, Colonel Higginson took no part in the service which was conducted by the village minister, Mr. George S. Dickerman, and their personal friend, the Reverend Jonathan Leavitt Jenkins, who pronounced the benediction. Emily's favorite chapter in 15th Corinthians was read. When the brief service was concluded, Colonel Higginson was asked to read the "Last Lines" of Emily Brontë's, beginning "No coward soul is mine." He prefaced his reading with a few remarks, saying that this was a favorite poem of Emily Dickinson who had just put on Immortality, "if she could ever have been said to have put it off." She often read this poem to her sister.

The poem was impressive and superbly read. When it ended at four o'clock, no hearse appeared at the outer door. Instead, the white coffin was placed upon a bier of pine boughs, so covered with sand violets that they swept the grass. The bier was raised on the shoulders of six faithful Irish workmen who had been laborers on the Dickinson grounds. All had had a profound reverence for Emily and they bore her across the fields filled with buttercups to the cemetery. It was a perfect spring day.

The immediate family followed the casket, and friends and neighbors who wished to go joined the procession. The grave was lined with green boughs and all the flowers, of which there were a profusion, were placed there with her. Vinnie had delegated most of the funeral arrangements to Sue Dickinson, knowing everything would be done in perfect taste and conducted according to Emily's wishes.

It was not until these sad days were finally over that Austin and Vinnie went to the mahogany bureau in Emily's room. Most of the letters were burned, but here they discovered many carefully sorted packets of poems, in Emily's delicate handwriting, all tied up very neatly with string. The brother and sister looked at each other and perhaps agreed that these could not be destroyed as the letters had been. They belonged to the world and should be preserved. They were part of Emily—her life's blood.

Let us think that Emily knew their devoted thoughts and was pleased.

Afterword

I T I S O N L Y F A I R for the readers of this book to expect a so-
lution to its mysteries—or at least to the big mystery of the
identity of the man Emily loved. I can only express and explain my conviction that Emily Dickinson's intense love of a
lifetime was Charles Wadsworth, the eloquent minister with
the deep voice.

Thirty years ago I was in Amherst at the home of Madame
Bianchi, Emily's niece and Austin's daughter, Martha. In a
talk with her companion and secretary, Alfred Leete Hampson, who knew everything about the Dickinson family, I
asked him to tell me who Emily's great love was.

He answered at once, "The man from Philadelphia—Wadsworth."

I was pleased, for this was the man I had chosen during a
study of Emily I was doing at the time. Emily may have flirted
with other men and been very fond of them, but once and
once only she renounced a great love, because Dr. Wadsworth was a married man.

The day of my visit to Amherst has never been forgotten

because I held in my own hands the packets of Emily's poems, as she had tied them with green-and-white butcher's string and put them away in her bureau in the room where Dr. Wadsworth's picture hung on the wall in an oval frame.

In past years, many have tried to unravel the threads in the life of Emily Dickinson. In future years, many more will try. Let us hope that somewhere, tucked away in some secure spot, are long forgotten letters that could help to solve the puzzle—and that someone who would recognize their value will find them.

Bibliography

Bianchi, Martha Dickinson. *Emily Dickinson Face to Face*. Unpublished Letters with Notes and Reminiscences. With a foreword by Alfred Leete Hampson. Archon Books, 1970. Houghton Mifflin Co., 192.

Bianchi, Martha Dickinson. *The Life and Letters of Emily Dickinson*. Boston: Houghton Mifflin Co., 1924.

Bingham, Millicent Todd. *Emily Dickinson*. A Revelation. New York: Harper & Brothers Publishers, 1954.

Bingham, Millicent Todd. *Emily Dickinson's Home*. Letters of Edward Dickinson and His Family. New York: Harper & Brothers Publishers, 1955.

Higgins, David. *Portrait of Emily Dickinson: The Poet and Her Prose*. New Brunswick, New Jersey: Rutgers University Press, 1967.

Johnson, Thomas Herbert. *Emily Dickinson: An Interpretive Biography*. Cambridge, Massachusetts: The Belknap Press of Harvard University Press, 1955.

Letters of Emily Dickinson. Edited by Mabel Loomis Todd. In two volumes. Boston: Roberts Brothers, 1894.

Letters of Emily Dickinson, The. Edited by Thomas H. Johnson. Associate editor Theodora Ward. 3 vols. Cambridge, Massachusetts: The Belknap Press of Harvard University Press, 1958.

Leyda, Jay. *The Years and Hours of Emily Dickinson.* 2 vols. New Haven: Yale University Press, 1960.

Longsworth, Polly. *Emily Dickinson: Her Letter to the World.* New York: T. Y. Crowell, 1965.

Poems by Emily Dickinson. Edited by two of her friends Mabel Loomis Todd and T. W. Higginson. Ser. 1-3. Boston: Roberts Bros., 1891–1896.

Pohl, Frederick J. *The Emily Dickinson Controversy.* Reprinted from the October Number of *The Sewanee Review,* 1933.

Walsh, John Evangelist. *The Hidden Life of Emily Dickinson.* New York: Simon and Schuster, 1971.

Ward, Theodora. *The Capsule of the Mind: Chapters in the Life of Emily Dickinson.* Cambridge, Massachusetts: The Belknap Press of Harvard University Press, 1961.

Wells, Anna Mary. *Dear Preceptor: The Life and Times of Thomas Wentworth Higginson.* Boston: Houghton Mifflin Co., 1963.

Whicher, George Frisbie. *This Was a Poet.* A Critical Biography of Emily Dickinson. New York: Charles Scribner's Sons, 1938.

Index

Index